The Write Mind
for Every Classroom

D1524134

The Write Mind
for Every Classroom

How to Connect Brain Science

and Writing Across the Disciplines

Jason Wirtz

ROWMAN & LITTLEFIELD
Lanham • Boulder • New York • London

Published by Rowman & Littlefield
A wholly owned subsidiary of The Rowman & Littlefield Publishing Group, Inc.
4501 Forbes Boulevard, Suite 200, Lanham, Maryland 20706
www.rowman.com

Unit A, Whitacre Mews, 26-34 Stannary Street, London SE11 4AB

British Library Cataloguing in Publication Information Available

Library of Congress Cataloging-in-Publication Data

ISBN 978-1-4758-1814-7 (hardback)
ISBN 978-1-4758-1815-4 (paperback)
ISBN 978-1-4758-1816-1 (e-book)

∞ The paper used in this publication meets the minimum requirements of
American National Standard for Information Sciences—Permanence of Paper for
Printed Library Materials, ANSI/NISO Z39.48-1992.

Printed in the United States of America

Contents

Acknowledgments

The author wishes to thank the following individuals for participating in the interview study at the heart of this book: Patrick Bizzaro, Deborah Brandt, Stuart Dybek, Peter Elbow, Mariah Fredericks, James Gee, Brenda Greene, Adam Higginbotham, George Irish, Elizabeth Kerlikowske, Yusef Komunyakaa, Janice Lauer, Andrea Lunsford, Art Markman, Richard Maxwell, Elizabeth Nunez, William Olsen, Mike Rose, Diane Seuss, Nancy Sommers, Robert Stickgold, Leora Tanenbaum, Diane Wakoski, and Gene Yang.

Gratitude is extended to: Hunter College for grants that have supported this research, including the CUNY Collaborative Incentive Research Grant Program (co-collaborator David Allen), the PSC-CUNY Research Award, the Presidential Fund for Faculty Advancement, and Travel Award Grants to present research; colleagues at Hunter College who have had to listen to me talk about the brain for the past couple of years—especially members of the executive committee: Karen Koellner, Jody Polleck, and Melissa Schieble Pirro; mentors and friends providing intellectual support over the years, including Patrick Bizzaro, Jonathan Bush, and Suzanne Nalbantian.

Finally, I would like to express appreciation to my wife, Brittany Wirtz, and immediate family members Suzanne Wirtz, Ken and Lynn Wirtz, Clinton Wirtz, and Deborah VanDenBrink. Special thanks to Van Clinton Wirtz, who advised on all aspects of this book related to superheroes and dinosaurs.

Foreword

Jonathan Bush
Professor of English Education and Writing Studies, Western Michigan University
Co-editor of *Teaching/Writing: The Journal of Writing Teacher Education* and co-author of *But Will It Work with Real Students: Scenarios for Teaching Secondary English Language Arts* (NCTE, 2003) and *Grammar to Enrich and Enhance Student Writing* (Heinemann, 2008).

I am pleased to have the opportunity to introduce this exciting and important book. The teaching of writing and, correspondingly, the education, training, and support of writing teachers have undergone a powerful and ongoing revolution that began in the 1960s and continues today. From early transitions from lore-based ideas and inconsistent practices and ideas, through process theories, cognitivism, socially relevant pedagogies and detailed understanding and consideration of audience, process, and genre, the teaching of writing has continued to advance, refine, and move forward, becoming more systematic and scholarly in the way it is approached and practiced.

As the field developed, a tradition of borrowing and adapting from other disciplines became normalized, becoming what Janice Lauer concluded should be called a "dappled discipline" with all the advantages and risks associated with such a concept. Regardless of these risks, it's hard to imagine a composition studies that didn't reach out beyond disciplinary borders. Much of our pedagogical and theoretical advancement has occurred in connection to humanism, of course, but there has always been a connection to scientific ideas and processes as well. Wirtz exemplifies this concept well, stating, "this book is about bringing together knowledge from the humanities—in this case—what we know about writing—with knowledge from the brain sciences."

As I read (and re-read) this text, I kept making notes to myself, both in the margins and on a notepad—both critiquing my own practices—learning from Wirtz and what he teaches us about composition and the brain sciences—and keeping tabs of core concepts that I wanted to practice in my writing classes. More importantly, I kept a running list of ideas that I felt needed to be communicated to my teacher education students—in many cases, blank slates in the field of composition and the teaching of writing—so that they could enhance their own teaching practices: brain states, theories of mind, emotional engagement, non-conscious cognition—among others. All these ideas—and more—enhance my current concepts of best practices in my classroom—both problematizing and engaging my teacherly perspective and helping me, and my future teachers, better visualize why student writers—and why all writers—do what they do.

Additionally, Wirtz also gave me new tools to re-read old texts. I have a new lens by which to reach canonical composition studies—works by Ede and Lunsford, Emig, and Sommers' study of student and experienced writer revision strategies, among many others. I have been able to re-read these, almost as new articles, and gain additional appreciation for what they teach me about writing and teaching. I feel as I now can re-read entire articles—especially those that focus on writer actions and decision-making—and gain new understandings about them through Wirtz's ideas. I think that this text will also help other readers to do the same reflection on their own work through this lens and also experience the theories and practices of composition studies through a new perspective.

The text is not only well researched and well positioned, but it is also practical and universal. Both a university instructor and an elementary teacher can read it, and both gain knowledge to better understand their practices and the needs of their students. Likewise, composition scholars and others in the humanities can gain perspective and insight about scientific thought and neuroscience as it relates to writing. Scientists can read the text and better understand the pedagogical perspectives of writing. It is a landmark book, one that I believe will become an important addition for anyone who wants to better understand pedagogy, writing, and the interaction with brain sciences.

And, Jason Wirtz is the perfect person to write this text. Composition studies has always been driven by scholars and teachers willing to reach into new fields of thought and exploration. He is an innovator and a seasoned teacher who looks at his own practice as a laboratory. And, as a researcher, teacher educator, and writer, he understands methodology, pedagogy, and the process of a working writing. He is also someone who has built a scholarly career of finding, building a close understanding of, and translating and explaining connections between complex concepts. This makes his writing style well organized and engaging and valuable for both experts and novices alike. There is much to learn from this text and I expect that it will become a staple of many teachers' libraries and essential readings collections.

Introduction

What makes the human brain remarkable? One word: *connections*. The human brain is made up of roughly a hundred billion neurons—as many stars as there are in the Milky Way—and each neuron can have up to ten thousand connections (Sousa, 2011). These connections provide the ladder to consciousness and enable such higher-order cognitive faculties as speaking, listening, viewing, and—the focus of this book—writing.

Learning about the brain inspires us to make our own connections. Bringing together knowledge from the humanities and sciences, for example, is a connection that can yield dynamic, three-dimensional perspectives. This book is about bringing together knowledge from the humanities—in this case, what we know about writing and the teaching of writing—with knowledge from the brain sciences.

Fundamental to this effort is the belief that any holistic perspective on writing and teaching writing must come from a convergence of disciplinary perspectives. This is the idea of consilience, the idea that the convergence of independent sources of information result in our greatest understandings (Wilson, 1999). I've always kept in mind this excerpt from the autobiography of none other than Charles Darwin (1887) when thinking about the importance of making connections between the humanities and sciences:

> I have said that in one respect my mind has changed during the last twenty or thirty years. . . . My mind seems to have become a kind of machine for grinding general laws out of large collections of facts . . . if I had to live my life again, I would have made a rule to read some poetry and listen to some

music at least once every week; for perhaps the parts of my brain now atrophied would thus have been kept active through use. The loss of these tastes is a loss of happiness. (82–83)

The humanist who purposefully avoids scientific methods and discoveries is apt to repeat this same mistake in reverse. Bringing together the two powerful cultures of the humanities and sciences is where our understanding of complex concepts—and writing and writing pedagogy are certainly complex—deepens and widens most effectively and creatively.

The final point I wish to make on this topic of generatively bridging the gap between the humanities and sciences is that educators are desperately needed to help accomplish this goal. As the evolutionary biologist and two-time Pulitzer prizewinner E. O. Wilson argues:

> There is only one way to unite the great branches of learning and end the culture wars. It is to view the boundary between the scientific and literary cultures not as a territorial line but as a broad and mostly unexplored terrain awaiting cooperative entry from both sides. The misunderstandings arise from ignorance of the terrain, not from a fundamental difference in mentality. (137)

Modern brain science is a field comprised of many converging disciplines such as physics, neurology, molecular biology, psychology, psychiatry, mathematics, philosophy, and—yes—education.

I encourage you to think of how your own thinking and teaching offers contributions to this new landscape that has been alternatively named *educational neuroscience* or *mind, brain, and education* (*MBE*). As these titles indicate, the experience of educators is central to the development and application of this burgeoning field.

THE RIGHT LEVEL OF DESCRIPTION

As part of my research for this book I interviewed Robert Stickgold about his writing habits and strategies. Stickgold is an ideal person to speak with about the overlap of writing and brain research because in addition to having published science fiction novels he is a neuroscience professor at Harvard where he specializes in sleep and cognition. Stickgold can speak to the experience of writing and the neural underpinnings involved. In our conversation he brought up an important point that bears repeating:

> If I told you the position and momentum of every quark and lepton in your brain, you would have complete knowledge of everything that's going on in your brain. . . . Then the brain is totally defined and that information is ab-

solutely useless because it's not a level of description that can even help you understand an acetylcholine receptor at a neuromuscular junction. Knowing the position of every electron in every atom in an acetylcholine receptor doesn't give you useful information. It's actually all the information you need, but it's at the wrong level of description.

So what is the right level of description? For our purposes of integrating brain research and writing pedagogy the right level of description is certainly not to describe the brain at the molecular or subatomic level. While there are parts of the brain that need describing we do not need to peer into that level of detail. Such descriptions would be distractions to the task at hand.

A primary reason I have been drawn to brain research is for its stories— scientifically valid stories that demonstrate research findings in ways that are engaging and memorable. These stories are the bridges that connect to writing and writing pedagogy, and so you will find that I consistently share stories from brain research to illustrate points about the brain and make connections to writing and the teaching of writing. This is the right level of description in order to evoke a synergistic relationship between brain research and writing.

WHO SHOULD READ THIS BOOK

First and foremost, and most inclusively, anyone fascinated by thinking and learning about connections between brain research and writing should read this book. I imagine that teachers of writing across a wide range of grade levels will find this book useful, especially those teaching adolescents.

The information and activities are designed for those teaching across secondary and postsecondary content areas. As writing becomes increasingly central across all content areas as a result of both federal and state mandates such as the Common Core State Standards (CCSS), this book will be useful to all teachers of adolescents.

College and university professors will find this book useful in helping to prepare today's preservice teachers. As someone who works with preservice teachers this is a particularly important group to me. My reason for writing this book stems in part from my desire to see a book that brings together what we know about writing across the disciplines with brain research.

Literacy coaches, principals, and mentor/lead teachers will find much of value, as will educators involved in teacher learning groups. As brain-based education enters the national spotlight it becomes increasingly important for educators at all levels to become intelligent consumers of brain-based claims that have a potentially far-reaching impact on student learning.

I have also made a concerted effort to highlight the areas where this consilient view of teaching writing can make strong connections with issues particularly relevant to educators today: CCSS, working with English Language Learners (ELLs), struggling student writers, and writers with disabilities.

OVERVIEW OF CHAPTERS

Chapter 1: Automaticity and Writing. An important concept in brain science, automaticity is the idea that automatic processes are created in the brain as a result of experience and practice. Several Student Writing Exercises are offered to take full advantage of this insight from brain science.

Chapter 2: Theory of Mind and Writing. Theory of mind is "the nature of our ability to understand and reason about the beliefs of others" (Siegal and Varley, 2002). This chapter extends the popular thinking that reading helps develop theory of mind by arguing that writing also strengthens the neuronal connections required of theory of mind processing. Activities designed to help adolescent writers conceptualize audience within the writing process are emphasized.

Chapter 3: Brain States and Writing. Our lives are complex dramas in which we must shift in and out of several states of mind. We can be a friend, mother, father, mentor, teacher, etc. And even within these roles we adopt various states of mind such as sympathetic or authoritative, as the situation calls for. Such brain states are significant to the writing process. Academic language is a central concept to be explored in this chapter and refers to the linguistic tools needed to imagine oneself as the kind of person who can use language to do science, math, or ethics, and who can become a person who takes on the role and identity of a scientist, mathematician, ethicist, etc. (Wilhelm, 2007).

Chapter 4: Brain Variation and Writing. No two brains function alike. Identical twins, for example, have different brains based on different life experiences actively shaping brain structure. The takeaway for educators is that adolescent writers learn differently and therefore instructional variation is vital. This chapter looks at impressive studies from brain science illustrating brain variation, which sets the stage for activities stressing differentiation in writing instruction. Working with English Language Learners (ELLs) and Learning Disabled (LD) students is highlighted in this chapter.

Chapter 5: Positive Affect and Writing. The evidence from brain science is clear: There is no learning without emotional engagement. This chapter illustrates the importance of emotional engagement to the writing process followed by activities to support adolescents in making personal connections to their writing.

Chapter 6: Nonconscious Cognition and Writing. A surprising finding of brain science is that, counter to our day-to-day lived reality of making conscious decision after decision, the vast majority of our cognitive processes are nonconscious. This chapter illustrates the predominance of nonconscious cognition before outlining an important intellectual stance, the receptive stance, designed to take full advantage of the many nonconscious cognitive functions germane to the writing process. This stance of receptivity is found in accomplished writers and should be cultivated in classrooms focused on writing instruction. Several specific strategies are offered to support adolescent writers.

Chapter 7: Bringing It All Together: The Metacognitive Writing Classroom. This concluding chapter brings together the central components of this book, arguing for a metacognitive writing classroom in which students and teachers alike are cognizant of the ways our brains interact with writing. This chapter focuses on strategies to help promote a metacognitive writing classroom in which brain science plays an inspirational and galvanizing role.

ADOLESCENCE AS A TIME OF ONGOING DEVELOPMENT

If the first overarching theme of this book is "sciences and humanities can work together to inform writing instruction," the second overarching theme is "adolescent brains are still highly malleable, which is a great thing for the teaching of writing." As a specialist in adolescent social behavior, Sarah-Jayne Blakemore (2012) describes how the adolescent brain is physically different from the adult and child brain. Understanding how the adolescent brain is different helps clarify this developmental period.

In adolescence the prefrontal cortex is still very much in development. The prefrontal cortex is linked with our cognitive abilities to make rational decisions, plan for the future, inhibit inappropriate behavior, engage in social interactions, and operate with a sense of self-awareness. Blakemore has confirmed through fMRI studies that the adolescent brain has more white matter and increasingly less gray matter. More white matter is a result of the strengthening of axons in the brain. Axons are strengthened as the myelin sheath encasing axons gets stronger. It is this myelin sheath that shows up white under a microscope. At the same time gray matter is lessening as a result of synaptic pruning—the elimination of unused synaptic connections.

All this provides a view of adolescence as an active developmental period in which the adolescent brain is shaping itself in response to social context. Rather than viewing adolescence as a time of great emotional and irrational upheaval, brain research encourages us to flip the problem on its head and view adolescent impulsivity as a sign of malleability. Adolescence is a time period when education is of paramount concern. Rather than the brain being mostly formed by the teenage years, as was previously believed, we now know the brain is highly plastic throughout adolescence and into early adulthood. Education during adolescence takes on an increasingly central role when viewed through the lens of brain research.

1

✛

Automaticity and Writing

INTRODUCTION AND CHAPTER OVERVIEW

In making connections between brain science and the teaching of writing, an essential fact continuously surfaces: Rather than replacing what educators know from experience is good practice, brain science supports what we already hold as good practice. The concept of automaticity from brain science is a wonderful example of this fact.

We will first take a look at what automaticity means from the scientific perspective. We will then look at automaticity from the humanistic perspective, hearing from accomplished writer-teachers. Several writing exercises for use with adolescent learners will be shared, writing exercises designed to capitalize on this concept of automaticity.

THE SCIENTIFIC VIEW OF AUTOMATICITY

The notion of creating automatic, habitual cognition has been around since at least the late 1800s when the prescient William James wrote about the importance of habit formation in his *Principles of Psychology*: "*We must make automatic and habitual, as early as possible, as many useful actions as we can,* and as carefully guard against the growing into ways that are likely to be disadvantageous. The more of the details of our daily life we can hand over to the effortless custody of automatism, the more our higher powers of mind will be set free for their own proper work" (122, italics original).

Contemporary brain science offers a striking study to illustrate auto-maticity at work in the brain. This study conducted with sixteen London taxi drivers with experience ranging from one and a half to forty-two years demonstrated that a part of the hippocampus responsible for spatial awareness was actually larger in those taxi drivers with more experience (Maguire et al., 2000). In other words, those drivers with the greatest experience navigating the London roadways actually grew larger brains in the location related to spatial awareness.

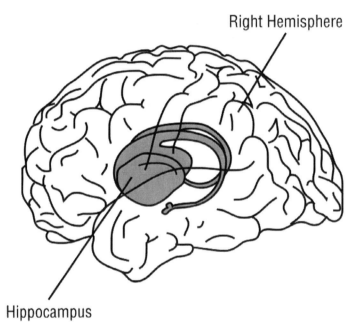

Figure 1.1. Location of the hippocampus in the brain found to be responsible for spatial awareness among other cognitive functions, such as the consolidation of short-term memory into long-term memory.

Another study illustrating such plasticity of the brain was conducted on dancers. This EEG study showed that professional dancers had greater brain synchronization than those of novice dancers, indicating that their brains patterned thought differently as a result of extensive dancing experience (Fink, Graif, and Neubauer, 2009). Similar studies have been conducted on stringed musicians (Ebert et al., 1995) and jazz musicians (Limb and Braun, 2008), demonstrating that practice and experience results in changes to brain architecture.

Examples of automaticity from everyday experience include typing, driving, swimming, riding a bicycle, even walking. All of these abilities require years of practice before they become ingrained, subsumed, automatic. How does something become automatic? Brain science answers this question with the concept of brain plasticity.

Plasticity references the brain's ongoing ability to alter its own architecture. Popular neuroscientist V. S. Ramachandran goes so far as to say, "We might as well call ourselves *Homo plasticus*," as we are "the only species to use [plasticity] as a central player in brain refinement and evolution" (2011, 38, italics original). The plasticity of the brain, its ability to strengthen and grow neuronal connections in response to external stimuli, is the physical manifestation of automaticity.

WRITER-TEACHERS SPEAK TO AUTOMATICITY

Mike Rose, an internationally recognized educator and writer at UCLA, speaks to this process of automaticity, referencing his own work on the subject:

> My book *The Mind at Work* really got me to think about this business of automaticity, what the cognitive scientists call it. Yes, and so if you think about any learned skill, whether it's being a defensive tackle on a football team or a dancer or a racecar driver or a surgeon or a skilled plumber, at the beginning stages all of this stuff is so very conscious and filled with concentration and trying to master these various moves and as you become more and more expert it becomes more and more routine and more and more just a part of the way you function so that your cognitive space, if you will, is freed up to do other things.

For many writers the most obvious role of automaticity is in the development of craft.

Poet William Olsen describes:

> I've read and written a lot. Poetry is an act of making as well as an act of seeing. In other words, it requires craft and one has to learn one's craft. You don't want to sit on a two-legged chair. I gave myself to learning that craft and now I can rely more on intuition.

Janice Lauer, a foremost scholar of writing studies, speaks to automatizing craft in detail using the example of skiing:

> I'm very convinced of the importance of—I don't like the word craft, I like the word art, I think of the Greek sense of *techne*—things that can be learned

and then the necessity of having learned them, one then sets them aside. I used to in talks in the very beginning when I was talking about invention I used to talk about champion skiers. I couldn't turn and I finally had a teacher who took parts of it, I was in a class, got us to understand that when you came to the point of turning you "lift, pull, turn" that was your little art and I learned to turn which was wonderful because I otherwise wouldn't have skied. But then for people who are mature, like people who are in ski championships if they started thinking about themselves when they came out on top they would probably fail because that's so second nature to them and I think that's the same way with writing. . . . And grammar of course and even genre conventions that those can be taught and learned so that when the student is in the act of writing they have learned and practiced some of these things and then they just do it smoothly and automatically.

As with many brain processes, automaticity shows itself most clearly in the borderlands, the places where it breaks down or just begins to work. Mike Rose asks the question: "What about those moments suddenly where—oh, this is kind of interesting—where a writer realizes that there's something they want to do and they need to learn more as to how to do it so they put the book down and they go read some people who do villanelles really well or something? Where you suddenly are aware that you want to be doing something that you're not really that skilled at it so suddenly you kick back into learning mode?"

Remarkably, my interview data has an answer for this line of inquiry, an answer highlighting the movement from deliberate practice to automaticity. Poet Elizabeth Kerlikowske shares this experience:

Two days ago, I have this book of forms, and I try these new forms and the Welsh ones are always unpronounceable and they're syllabic and they rhyme so I wrote a poem in this form and it was not my best poem but once I can wrap my head around the form it's cool. So then today when I went to rewrite a different poem I rewrote it according [to] the way I thought it should sound but it was in the form of the Welsh poem, unintentional, but I had absorbed it and there it was presented back to me without my even knowing it.

Gene Yang, most well known as author of the graphic novels *American Born Chinese* and *Boxers & Saints*, speaks to the process of automaticity as moving from your brain to your gut: "I think that you have to learn it and then forget it, and then so that it sinks in. It goes from your brain to your gut. The things that you wrote in your brain end up in your gut and that's what could create an authentic story."

The concept of automaticity is a border crosser as scientists, educators, and writers speak to its central role in cognitive processes such as driving, dancing, skiing, and of course writing.

AUTOMATICITY AND TEACHING WRITING

Now that we've viewed the concept of automaticity from both scientific and humanistic perspectives we can make connections to the teaching of writing. What do writing exercises look like when grounded in an understanding of automaticity as foundational to the way our brains work? There are three major guideposts to keep in mind.

1. Adolescents need opportunities to *write a lot*. Automaticity tells us that extensive writing practice is the brain-changer that helps adolescent writers automatize writing processes.
2. Adolescents need opportunities to *practice good writing*. Automaticity tells us that practice doesn't make perfect; practice makes permanent. What adolescents practice in their writing is what will become automatic.
3. Adolescents are empowered when they are *aware of how automatic writing habits develop*. A better understanding of these automatized elements can aid both student and teacher.

WRITING ACTIVITIES ENCOURAGING ADOLESCENTS TO WRITE A LOT

These writing activities seek to maximize the output of adolescent writers to take full advantage of the brain process of automaticity.

Writer's Notebook

The writer's notebook is a staple in all of my writing classrooms. The idea is simple: Students need to fill a certain amount of pages within a certain amount of time. (I find that thirty pages a month works well.) At the end of the month I gather the notebooks in class while students are working on something independently and simply count the number of pages they have written and provide a grade accordingly.

What are students writing? First and foremost: whatever they want. You can even tell students they can copy the dictionary if they choose. (It becomes immediately apparent that copying the dictionary is actually more difficult than simply writing about whatever topic comes to mind.) It also works well to have students use their *Writer's Notebooks* during class time to complete shorter writing assignments such as freewrites and responding to questions since the students are happy to complete an activity that also helps them meet their monthly page quota.

Also, don't grade everything! A major obstacle to integrating more writing into the classroom is that the amount of time spent grading can skyrocket. It's important to keep in mind that not everything students write must be graded. In fact, if you are grading everything your students write then your students are not writing enough.

The *Writer's Notebook* is a great example of an activity helping to maximize student writing. Students are writing thirty pages a month and all you have to do is count the number of pages written. Additionally, a goal in any writing classroom is that students develop intrinsic rather than extrinsic motivation to write. Providing opportunities for students to practice their writing free from the eyes of the teacher can help enable the development of such intrinsic motivators.

Other useful strategies of non-grading include having students write three responses to a writing prompt and then have them choose one of the three to be graded or "turned in." Another strategy is to have students write to an audience other than the teacher. When the audience changes to a peer or family member, for example, there is no need for the teacher to be reading and grading the writing beyond checking to see if it has been completed. An underlying goal here is to maximize student writing while minimizing in smart, efficient ways teacher involvement.

Writing When Not Writing

We know that "binge writers"—those that write for long hours sporadically—do not write as much or as well as writers who write in smaller increments of time but consistently. "Writing when not writing" seeks to take advantage of this by integrating short writing assignments throughout the curriculum. These are not overt writing activities but nevertheless help to integrate writing into everyday curriculum. Here are some examples of writing-rich activities that can be integrated across all content areas:

- *K-W-L (What do you Know? What do you Want to know? What have you Learned?)*: This is a popular activity usually centered around a piece of reading although it works just as well with an activity such as a lab in a science classroom or a new concept to be covered in mathematics, social studies, or foreign language. It's a three-step process in which students first write down what they already know about the reading or topic followed by what they want to know. After the reading or lesson is complete, students return to write about what they have learned.
- *Q&A*: This is similar to *K-W-L* in that it focuses on writing before a reading or lesson followed by writing after a reading or lesson. In this

case students are asked to write out a number of Questions and then, following the reading or lesson, pick a few of these questions to now Answer based on what they have learned.

- *Write/Pair/Share*: This quick activity asks students to write individually in response to a question or prompt and then pair up with a partner to share. This can then segue into sharing with the whole class. The activity is meant to scaffold toward sharing with a larger audience as adolescents first work individually then share with a partner and then with the whole class.

- *Translation*: This works particularly well in mathematics and science classrooms. Have students explain an equation or concept in writing. For example, students could be asked to explain *pi* in their own words. The mathematical explanation of pi includes the idea that pi is equal to the diameter of a circle divided by the circumference. Having students explain this beyond the equation alone helps them to conceptualize and confirm their understanding.

- *Written Conversation*: This activity gets students writing a lot. Here's how it works: The only rule is that there should be no talking. Divide the class into smaller groups of three to five students. Have each student start with a blank piece of paper on which they write out a question pertaining to the lesson or reading. Each student then passes the paper clockwise and reads the question posed by another student.

Students then have a choice to, in writing, respond to the question or ask another question. Students then pass the paper again, reading both responses this time before writing a response or asking a new question. This pattern is repeated until everyone in the group has written to everyone else (i.e., until the original author gets her paper back).

There are many benefits to this exercise. First, students are writing a lot and they are writing to each other for the sake of earnest communication. Second, the teacher can collect these and have a record of the conversation (oral conversations, while engaging, cannot be captured in this manner). Third, this written conversation exercise requires every student to get involved, something oral conversations often lack. Finally, this exercise always serves as a primer for a great oral conversation. After writing the conversation students are eager to talk about their experiences and what they've both read and written.

- *In Your Own Words*: This is a closure activity in which students are asked to write, in their own words, what they've learned. It can be numbered such as: "Write three things you've learned" or it can be open-ended such as: "Tell me, in your own words, what you've learned."

- *Exit Slips*: This is a popular closure activity and can be modified to best fit the context of instruction. Exit slips are usually half sheets of paper written on at the end of a lesson (before students exit the classroom) prompting a written reflection. An exit-slip prompt, for example, might be: "Write down one new thing you've learned today, one question you still have, and one thing you are still unsure or confused about." Closure activities such as *In Your Own Words* and *Exit Slips* are formative, ungraded assessments providing a snapshot of student understanding that informs future instruction.
- *13 Ways of Looking*: The name of this writing activity, *13 Ways of Looking*, comes from the Wallace Stevens poem *Thirteen Ways of Looking at a Blackbird*. This highly anthologized poem is a literal list of thirteen ways to view a blackbird. What becomes evident in Stevens's poem is that the task of describing a blackbird in thirteen different ways is remarkably inventive.

In translating this to writing instruction, have students come up with thirteen (or any other number of) ways of describing an essential component of a lesson. For example, students come up with a list of thirteen ways that they use mathematics in their everyday lives or thirteen ways of viewing a historical figure they are studying.

There are at least four distinct advantages to this activity. First, this activity highlights variety as students are encouraged to view an object, person, or idea in multiple ways. Second, it encourages perspective taking as students are encouraged to view this object, person, or idea from the vantages of others. Third, this activity pushes students beyond their initial impressions toward deeper thinking. Lastly, in keeping with the principals of writing more to promote the further development of automatic writing skills, this activity pushes students to describe something in thirteen different ways rather than in one or two.

WRITING ACTIVITIES SUPPORTING GOOD WRITING

These writing activities, rather than maximizing writing output, seek to slow the writing down and have adolescents pay close attention to the quality of the writing.

Sentence Combining

Sentence combining is an activity wherein students are given a series of short sentences and are asked to combine the sentences to create longer, complex sentence structures. Sentence combining can be done individually, in pairs, or in small groups. Table 1.1 shows an example with the sentence-combining prompt on the left and an adolescent response on the right:

Table 1.1.

Sentence-Combining Prompt	Adolescent Writer Response
Blake woke in the middle of the night. He wasn't feeling well. He got up and walked to the store for some medicine. The store was closed. There was a light on in the back of the store. Blake knocked on the glass door. The glass broke. The alarm went off. He heard sirens in the distance.	Blake looked over at the clock; it was nearly 2am. His muscles were aching and his head was throbbing. He rolled out of bed, dragged himself to the medicine cabinet but it was empty. Realizing he had to go out into the cold for medicine, he started to second guess whether he was really sick. When a wave of pain rolled over him, he relented himself to the fact and got dressed. When he finally arrived, to his horror, the doors were locked but he saw a solitary light at the back of the store. Holding onto a faint glimmer of hope, he knocked. The glass shattered before him and almost simultaneously the alarms started blaring. In the next second, police sirens started up from down the block.

In combining sentences adolescent writers are encouraged to add description and detail and even more action or content to their writing. Adolescents enjoy sharing their finished products and hearing or reading what peers have done with the same sentence-combining prompt.

Teacher Talk-Aloud

Modeling best practices is a strategy to have adolescents practice good writing. Modeling note-taking strategies and paraphrasing skills are two examples of writing skills needed across content areas that students must learn. *Teacher Talk-Aloud* is a strategy wherein the teacher demonstrates a writing practice while talking through the process to illustrate the decision-making involved. An important and necessary step is to have adolescent writers practice the writing skills modeled after the *Teacher Talk-Aloud*.

Apprentice Writing

Accomplished writers from every genre of writing utilize *Apprentice Writing* as a strategy. In this strategy writers "try out" another author's writing along a spectrum from direct copying to viewing another writer's work as a loose example or inspiration. *Apprentice Writing*—having students dissect, copy, or replicate a piece of writing by substituting some of their own language—works when the writing task has a readily identifiable form such as with the lab report, abstract, character analysis, five-paragraph essay, thesis statement, business letter, etc.

Apprentice Writing highlights the importance of genre, which supports the development of academic language. In addition to trying on the vocabulary of a given discipline, *Apprentice Writing* teaches syntax, the order of information provided within a certain discipline and genre.

A popular *Apprentice Writing* activity is the "Where I'm From" poem by George Ella Lyon. Figure 1.2 shows an *Apprentice Writing* activity based on Lyon's poem.

Where I'm From (Template)

I am from _____ (specific ordinary item),
from _____ (product name) and _____.
I am from the _____ (home description...
adjective, adjective, sensory detail).
I am from the _____ (plant, flower, natural
item), the _____ (plant, flower, natural detail)
I am from _____ (family tradition) and
_____ (family trait), from _____ (name of
family member) and _____ (another family
name) and _____ (family name).
I am from the _____ (description of family
tendency) and _____ (another one).
From _____ (something you were told as a
child) and _____ (another).
I am from (representation of religion, or lack of
it). Further description.
I'm from _____ (place of birth and family
ancestry), _____ (two food items representing
your family).
From the _____ (specific family story about a
specific person and detail), the _____ (another
detail, and the _____ (another detail about
another family member).
I am from _____ (location of family pictures,
mementos, archives and several more lines
indicating their worth).

Figure 1.2.

MAPS

MAPS is an acrostic designed to help remind adolescents to think through the "big ideas" of any writing project. The idea behind *MAPS* is teachers cannot prepare adolescent writers for every writing encounter they will face; however, if adolescents are given the skills to unpack the needs of any given writing event for themselves then they are empowered to teach themselves how to properly respond to any given writing event.

MAPS is designed to help adolescent writers "map" out their approach to a writing project by breaking down the writing project into four essential questions: (1) What is the Mode? (2) Who is the Audience? (3) What is the Purpose behind the writing? (4) What is the Situation of the writing project?

Here is further explication of these four essential elements:

- Mode: This refers to the genre or format the writing is expected to take. A business letter takes on a different look and tone than an e-mail to a friend or lab report, for example. Adolescents need practice identifying the various modes of writing projects.
- Audience: Adolescents are in a critical period beginning to view the world from perspectives other than their own. Conceptualizing audience in their writing is a difficult yet essential writing skill for adolescents to develop. For example, adolescents have a tendency to write the name of someone—a close friend or relative—and not realize that their readers do not have access to all the information about this person. Adolescent writers need practice thinking through the experiences of their readers.
- Purpose: Beyond "getting a good grade," adolescents need to think through what they want their writing to accomplish. Are they seeking to be persuasive, descriptive, reflective? Identifying purpose enables adolescent writers to plan for the type of language, tone, and perspective they will adopt in their writing.
- Situation: There are two aspects of situation—the situation of the writing and the situation of the writer. The situation of the writing refers to the logistics around the writing project such as due date, length, and formatting guidelines. The situation of the writer is a rich metacognitive space in which students need to become more aware of their own tendencies as writers.

The big question for adolescent writers to consider is: "Under what conditions do I write best?" Once adolescents are aware of what conditions aid their writing process they are in a position to help create and maintain those conditions for themselves.

Adolescent writers may find they do their best writing in the morning, in the evening, with soft music playing, using specific pens, fonts, printing pages out for revision, having specific types of food and drink available, sharing with certain trusted readers, etc. Endless are the situations adolescent writers can discover and create for themselves to construct their best writing situations.

WRITING ACTIVITIES TO RECOGNIZE AUTOMATICITY AT WORK

Adolescent writing performance is enhanced by metacognitive understanding. These writing activities are designed to help adolescent writers better understand the role automaticity plays in their writing development.

Writing outside the Classroom

The cognitive process of automaticity is not restricted to the classroom. In fact, writing completed outside the classroom often best illustrates automaticity. Writing events such as text messaging, informal e-mailing, social networking—in brief, much of what adolescents write daily—are generative places to mine for evidence of automaticity at work.

Writing outside the Classroom is an activity where adolescents are asked to bring in exceptional examples of writing from outside the classroom. These examples can include text messages, informal e-mails, blog posts, social networking posts, Internet memes, etc. Students are then asked to share these exceptional examples with the whole class in pairs or small groups, explaining what makes them exceptional.

The idea behind *Writing outside the Classroom* is that adolescents have already automatically developed an understanding of what makes good, persuasive, descriptive writing within these contexts. Surfacing what they already know is a way to consciously uncover and review what has already become ingrained, automatic knowledge, and successfully transfer this knowledge to more academic domains.

Rubrics

Rubrics can clearly be useful to both teachers and adolescent writers. A rubric is an heuristic that breaks down a complex writing assignment into more manageable parts for both the teacher and the adolescent writer. Rubrics, at their best, create a document that acts as contract, communicating clearly the expectations of an assignment. Adolescent writers are

	Excellent	Good	Competent	Weak	Serious Problems
	A	B	C	D	F
A. **RESPONSE TO THE TOPIC** Writes an essay that is a substantial response to the question or topic and that includes a thesis statement and central focus.					
B. **EVIDENCE AND REASONING** Supports the thesis statement by drawing on relevant and substantial evidence. Avoids logical fallacies and unsupportable claims.					
C. **ORGANIZATION** Begins with an effective introduction and develops logical sequencing of ideas leading to a clear conclusion.					
D. **FLUENCY** Includes a variety of sentence types along with smooth and clear transitions within and across paragraphs.					
E. **GRAMMAR** Demonstrates knowledge of grammar conventions at the sentence level such as correct verb forms, sentence boundaries, and tense consistency.					
F. **MECHANICS** Controls mechanical conventions such as spelling, capitalization, punctuation, and formatting.					
G. **LANGUAGE AND WORD CHOICE** Uses language and vocabulary appropriate to the topic, genre, audience, and purpose.					
H. **CITATION** Incorporates ideas from and makes references to other texts using quotations and paraphrases and cites sources properly using correct documentation formatting. (Could be N/A-not applicable)					

Figure 1.3.

happy because they know what is expected of them; teachers are happy because rubrics can alleviate a lot of the subjectivity that accompanies the grading of writing assignments.

The weaknesses or downside to rubrics is that they can reduce a writing assignment into a type of checklist. The overreliance on rubrics can transform writing assignments into glorified to-do lists. Since rubrics dictate what a successful writing assignment should look like, they also have a tendency to limit creativity and the type of exploratory writing that comes when the writer is writing herself into unknown territory.

	Excellent A	Good B	Competent C	Fair D	Serious Problems F
A. RESPONSE TO THE TOPIC Writes an essay that is a substantial response to the question or topic and that includes a thesis statement and central focus.	Complex and/or creative response Strong focus throughout	Good response with thesis statement and clear focus	Some response to topic. Has thesis statement and focus, but also some tangents	Response, incoherent, unclear thesis or focus Few connections	Does not respond to assignment, Unfocused
B. EVIDENCE Supports the thesis statement by drawing on relevant and substantial evidence.	Evidence appropriate, explained, incorporated & mix of types	Evidence appropriate, not always explained, some missing explanations	Limited evidence, explanations missing, unincorporated	Little evidence, rarely, mostly of one type, not explained or analyzed	Assertions, not evidence and/or redundant
C. ORGANIZATION Begins with an effective introduction and develops logical sequencing of ideas leading to a clear conclusion	Smooth flow with transitions plus coherent Intro sets up conclusion with context	Mostly smooth flow, some transitions Topic sentences Good intro Basic conclusion	Ps out of place, few transitions Ps have tangents Intro of topic, not thesis Weak conclusion	Collection of Ps on a related topic, not a coherent essay	Fragmented ideas, not a coherent essay, nor coherent paragraphs
D. FLUENCY Includes a variety of sentence types along with smooth and clear transitions and signal phrases used within and across paragraphs.	Mix of sentence types, lengths Complex syntax Mix of P lengths	Some variation in P length, Some mix of compound, complex, sentences	Basic PIE (Point, Illustration, Explanation) paragraph structure, Few complex sentences, Syntax problems	Sentence level below college level, poor syntax	Overly simple sentence structure, below grade level
E. GRAMMAR Demonstrates knowledge of grammar conventions at the sentence level such as correct verb forms, sentence boundaries, and tense consistency.	Few if any errors	Some errors, which do not impede comprehension	More errors, some of which are confusing	Many errors, many types of errors Difficult to read	Grammar issues make paper very difficult to understand
F. MECHANICS Controls mechanical conventions such as spelling, capitalization, punctuation, and formatting.	Few if any errors MLA MS format correct	Spellcheck errors, some MS format problems	General control of mechanics, but uses Word defaults instead of MLA	Shows little understanding of mechanics, Odd formatting	Unacceptable formatting and/or punctuation problems
G. LANGUAGE AND WORD CHOICE Uses language and vocabulary appropriate to the topic, genre, audience, and purpose.	Appropriate key words Good use of academic language and awareness of audience	Straightforward language, used correctly, few if any inappropriate words	Generally straightforward lang, some incorrect, some inappropriate words and/or clichés	Frequent inappropriate word choice or dependence on jargon and/or clichés	Word choices make paper confusing to read
H. CITATION Incorporates ideas from and makes references to other texts using quotations and paraphrases and cites sources using appropriate documentation formatting. (Could be N/A-not applicable)	All paraphrases & quotes attributed. Cites everything in correct format	All paraphrases & quotes attributed. Citing generally correct.	Cites most sources with basic info and with occasional formatting problems	Many missing citations Problems with quotes and/or paraphrases.	Serious problems with quotes & paraphrasing Many missing or incorrect citations

Figure 1.4.

The takeaway here is that rubrics can be incredibly useful in a classroom focusing on writing instruction but they should not be used for every writing assignment. Rubrics, as a general rule, are more appropriate for WTSL (Writing To Show Learning) rather than WTL (Writing To Learn) activities. Another important takeaway is that rubrics always exist along a spectrum from being a guidepost to acting as a prescription for writing.

There are two basic types of rubrics—those that provide open-ended categories and those that provide categories with descriptions. Figure 1.3 is an example of a rubric with open-ended categories.

As you can see, the open-ended rubric is designed so that the student, teacher, or both can choose a grade among several categories and provide an explanation or rationale. A rubric with categories plus descriptions looks similar except more information is provided as the descriptions of what warrants each grade in each category are described. Figure 1.4 is the same open-ended rubric now completed with descriptions.

Adolescent-Created Rubrics

This strategy has students create their own rubric for a given assignment. This strategy is designed to serve two important purposes:

1. Adolescents think through their own expectations of what would be a successful response to the given writing assignment. This task further develops metacognition around writing by asking adolescent writers to surface their already held, automatized assumptions and beliefs about what makes for good writing.
2. In reviewing what students already believe about good writing and, more specifically, the successful ingredients of a given writing assignment, teachers can better assess what students understand and do not understand.

Something Old and Something New

This is a writing strategy in which adolescent writers compare and contrast two different pieces of their own writing from different time periods—an older piece of writing from last year or a few months ago and a current piece of writing. Such comparison helps adolescent writers to not only recognize what may be missing or weak in their earlier writing but to realize the automatized gains they have made in the interim. It is always encouraging to discover skills and strategies that have become "second nature" or automatic in one's writing process.

Leora Tanenbaum is an author who speaks directly to this idea of revisiting earlier writing and seeing more flaws, recognizing her own development over time:

I think I've become a better writer over time, experienced with it. I don't think—I don't think it is—for me, I don't think it has anything to do with the quality. I think I—when I read *Slut!*, I cringe. I can't even read it. I think the writing is really—I think the thinking is sloppy, and I was like, "Oy, if I could do it again, I would change everything," and then I go through each book, and I just—I find the writing stronger and stronger and stronger. I think that's just my cognitive development, my literary development, experience, just being older and wiser. I just think that I get stronger.

AUTOMATICITY AND WRITING: CONNECTIONS TO THE ENGLISH LANGUAGE ARTS WRITING COMMON CORE STATE STANDARDS

Developing automaticity within your adolescent writers is in alignment with Common Core State Standards (CCSS). The purpose of automaticity is to make habitual and automatic good writing strategies such as those within the CCSS. Here are a few ways the strategies in this chapter align with CCSS:

Writer's Notebook and *Writing When Not Writing* strategies connect with the CCSS call for: "Range of Writing: Write routinely over extended time frames (time for reflection and revision) and shorter time frames (a single sitting or a day or two) for a range of discipline-specific tasks, purposes, and audiences" (CCSS.ELA-Literacy.WHST.11-12.10). *Writer's Notebook* is a purposefully flexible strategy that targets writing "routinely over extended time frames."

Writer's Notebook can also be used to target "discipline-specific tasks, purposes, and audiences." *Writing When Not Writing* strategies are also varied and flexible and meet the CCSS call for writing within "shorter time frames (a single sitting or a day or two)."

Sentence Combining is a writing strategy that focuses in on complex and varied sentence construction. As a result, this strategy is ideal for the CCSS call to: "Use varied transitions and sentence structures to link the major sections of the text, create cohesion, and clarify the relationships among complex ideas and concepts" (CCSS.ELA-Literacy.WHST.11-12.2.C).

The CCSS are a shift toward writing with an emphasis on "arguments focused on discipline-specific content" and "informative/explanatory texts." *Teacher Talk-Aloud*, *Apprentice Writing*, and the use of *Rubrics* are strategies that allow a focus on the particulars of argumentative and informative/explanatory writing. A *Teacher Talk-Aloud*, for example, might demonstrate the construction of "a concluding statement or section that follows from or supports the argument presented." After the *Teacher*

Talk-Aloud adolescent writers could then practice constructing their own concluding statements in small groups or individually.

The use of *Rubrics* is a particularly proficient strategy to meet CCSS since language from the standards can be written directly into a rubric. For example, this standard: "Introduce precise, knowledgeable claim(s), establish the significance of the claim(s), distinguish the claim(s) from alternate or opposing claims, and create an organization that logically sequences the claim(s), counterclaims, reasons, and evidence" (CCSS. ELA-Literacy.WHST.11-12.1.A) can be migrated into a rubric that visually parses the four tasks being called for:

1. Introduction with thesis/argument;
2. Body paragraphs with evidence in support of thesis/argument;
3. Counterclaims;
4. Organizational structure with logical sequence.

Rubrics can be constructed around each of the Common Core writing standards.

WHERE WE'VE BEEN AND WHERE WE'RE GOING

This chapter provides an explanation of the brain's cognitive process of automaticity. The suggested activities for adolescent writers are designed to take full advantage of understanding how automatic skills develop in the brain.

The next chapter, *Theory of Mind and Writing*, introduces the concept of theory of mind before presenting activities designed to aid the development of theory of mind cognitive processes for adolescent writers.

2

✛

Theory of Mind and Writing

INTRODUCTION AND CHAPTER OVERVIEW

Theory of mind offers a rich place of consilience between the humanities and sciences. This chapter explains the concept of theory of mind from the perspective of brain science and from the perspective of writer-teachers of writing. Following these explanations several activities are presented and described, activities designed to make the successful transition from theory of mind as a cognitive concept to theory of mind as a set of integrated classroom practices for adolescent writers.

THE SCIENTIFIC VIEW OF THEORY OF MIND

The father of an autistic boy gained valuable insight into his son's thinking while watching him through a window. The boy was alone inside the house and could not know he was being observed. Standing in the center of the room, the boy pointed toward the cupboard where cookies were kept. After pointing for five, ten, and then fifteen minutes, he eventually deteriorated into a full-scale tantrum.

The boy did not understand pointing to what he wanted was a way of communicating with others; to his understanding, pointing was the act—akin to flipping a light switch—that produced his reward, not the adults who recognized his pointing and acted on his behalf. As a result of his autism the boy had difficulties conceptualizing other people's thinking.

From the scientific view it is said his autism adversely affected his theory of mind.

Theory of mind references our ability to know what is going on in other people's minds, to reason about the beliefs of others and ourselves. Theory of mind is a complex, interweaving set of cognitive structures fundamental to creativity, empathy, perspective taking, and effective communication.

As we have seen through the work of Sarah-Jayne Blakemore, adolescence is a time of ongoing cognitive development. This is true of the faculties associated with theory of mind. While simple tasks demonstrating theory of mind are successfully completed by ages four or five, more complex tasks associated with theory of mind suggest ongoing, continuing maturation well into adolescence and early adulthood. If you've spent time with adolescents you can likely attest that this is indeed a developmental period marked by alternating moods of sustained egocentrism alongside consistent efforts to understand the perspectives of others, especially peers.

An fMRI study conducted with twelve children and twelve adults illustrates the continual development of theory of mind (Pfeifer, Lieberman, and Dapretto, 2007). In this study the children and adults were placed in the fMRI scanner to measure brain activity while being asked to consider several phrases. As each phrase was read aloud the participants were asked to answer yes or no as to whether the phrase described oneself or a familiar fictional character—in this case, Harry Potter. Sample phrases included: "I am popular," "I wish I had more friends," "I like to read just for fun," and "Writing is so boring."

This experimental design displayed brain activity related to thinking about the mind of another (i.e., Does this phrase describe Harry Potter?) and the mind of oneself (i.e., Does this phrase describe you?). The self-knowledge category determined the brains of the children were much more active in both intensity and spatial extent than the adults in an area of the brain known as the medial prefrontal cortex.

This increased activity tells us the children were actually thinking harder and less efficiently than the adults when trying to decide if a phrase described themselves. In other words, the children had not reached a state of automaticity in which they knew themselves well enough to answer easily and efficiently. Their self-knowledge was still very much in development. The adults, in contrast, displayed more efficient, focused patterns of neural activity in the fMRI scanner, demonstrating that self-knowledge had become automatized.

The takeaway here is that adolescence, the period between childhood wherein self-knowledge is demonstrably less automatized than in adult-

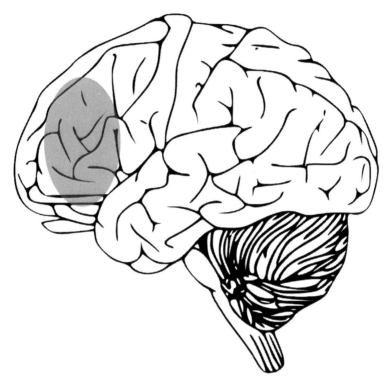

Figure 2.1. Location of the medial prefrontal cortex known to be linked to self-knowledge.

hood, is a period of ongoing development around theory of mind—the theorizing of other minds and one's own mind.

WRITER-TEACHERS SPEAK TO THEORY OF MIND

If the scientific perspective tells us cognitive faculties associated with theory of mind continue into adolescence and early adulthood, interviews with writer-teachers tell us the intellectual work associated with theory of mind continues well into adulthood and in fact never reaches a stopping point as such cognitive faculties are continuously refined.

Attending to audience is the writer's equivalent to theory of mind. Attending to audience involves actively invoking the beliefs and perspectives of one's audience while writing. Mike Rose speaks to the central role audience plays within his writing process, saying, "I am somebody who really does carry a lot of audiences around in my head by now. As I'm writing something I will find myself asking myself: 'How would so-and-so read this?'"

William Olsen says, "When writing you are choosing your own company. You're saying today my friend will be this writer and this writer and this writer." It is clear that accomplished writers are adept at invoking various audiences throughout the writing process.

It is also clear that accomplished writers continue to develop self-knowledge through writing as they position themselves as audience. Andrea Lunsford says, "Writing gives me insight into myself and my relations with other people" and Patrick Bizzaro says, "I think writing gives me understanding. But there's more. It gives me a kind of understanding that leads me away from myself and into other realms of knowing. In that sense, writing expands my identity."

When writing, these accomplished writers are choosing their audience based on the needs and situation of the given writing event. At times these writers invoke outside audiences in order to see their writing from a new perspective, a perspective other than their own. Other times it becomes essential to write for oneself, to invoke the self as audience.

THEORY OF MIND AND TEACHING WRITING

While the cognitive processes involved in theory of mind are most certainly interrelated and recursive, it becomes useful to parse theory of mind into these two categories for the sake of translating to the teaching of writing: (1) writing to learn and (2) writing to show learning.

Audience is the common denominator across these two categories. In writing-to-learn activities the audience is the author. Writing-to-learn activities are focused on the writer communicating with the self to pursue ideas without censure. Writing to learn focuses on freeing the author from constraints as these writing activities are designed to provide the writer with room to consider, question, and play.

In writing-to-show-learning activities the audience is other. Writing to show learning deliberately invokes outside audiences (most often in the mind but sometimes in person) to view the writing through another's perspective.

As a flexible rule, writing-to-learn activities most often provide starting points for the final writing product and thus serve as precursor to writing-to-show-learning activities. As the purpose of writing to learn is to construct a judgment-free zone for adolescent writers to think openly via writing, these activities are usually ungraded, or are simply given credit for completion. Writing-to-show-learning activities, by contrast, are designed to aid students in crafting writing to be shared with an audience and are therefore appropriate for assessment.

WRITING TO LEARN: THE SELF AS AUDIENCE

- *Freewriting.* A spectacularly popular writing-to-learn activity for good reason, freewriting should be a staple in any classroom emphasizing writing instruction. The way it works is simple: Writers are asked to write continuously for a set period of time, usually around five to ten minutes. The key component of this task is that writers are to write without stopping. Even if they can't think of anything to write, they should just write that: "I can't think of anything to write." Grammar, sentence structure, legibility—these concerns are all ignored as the writer is left to simply get ideas down on the page.

Freewriting is a powerful tool emphasizing writing as a tool for thought and expression. Too often writing is conceived as a medium for presenting ideas already held in mind. Freewriting demonstrates the usefulness of writing as a tool for surfacing and discovering ideas.

Freewriting can be used successfully at any point in a lesson from class discussion primers to closure activities. Freewrites can also be open-ended in nature or be given in response to a given stimulus. A physics teacher, for example, starts his classes daily with a question projected at the front of the room. "What will happen when Steve tries to step from his floating canoe onto the dock? Will he make it? Why or why not?" A question like this gets students to access their prior experiential knowledge which can then be used to make connections to the new knowledge to be covered, in this case new knowledge about how friction works (or does not work, in this case).

An important element of freewriting is what writers do with their freewrites when they've finished. I've found it useful in my own classrooms to have students go back and read their freewrites, highlighting or underlining some ideas of phrases they want to remember. Freewrites often prime students to want to share and discuss what they have written about. Another variation is to freewrite in response to a freewrite. This activity has adolescent writers pick out an idea or two from their original freewrite to explore in a second freewriting session.

- *Double-Entry Reading Notes.* This is an effective writing-to-learn strategy constructed around a reading assignment. Have adolescent writers fold the notebook page horizontally to create two columns (this can easily be done on a computer screen as well). The columns create a "double-entry" system of note taking with guiding questions or quotations on one side and personal observations or connections on the other. The idea here is that there can be more structured notes on the left side of the page while leaving the right side of the page open to writing-to-learn jottings and notes stemming from the reading.

- *Delay the Prompt.* Experiment with having adolescent writers spend time writing before they are given the actual writing prompt. The delivery of the writing prompt immediately begins to shape the writer and writing around the final writing deliverable, therefore delaying the prompt creates space to explore before the work of organizing toward a finished product.

As an example, before asking her students to write an essay explaining digestion, one science teacher had her students write several short reaction statements to the following activities:

1. Each student is given a saltine cracker to describe in detail what happens as they eat the cracker. This elicits the difference between physical and chemical digestion.
2. Students are asked to consider what would happen if they were to eat the cracker while standing on their heads. Students were then asked to describe the way toothpaste containers work. These reaction statements are aimed toward understanding the concept of peristalsis.
3. Students are asked to fold a piece of paper accordion style and write about the relationship between surface area and space. Just like the intestines, which contain folds to occupy less space while maintaining surface area, the folded paper accomplishes the same task.
4. Students are asked to respond to the question: "Why is it important to eat your vegetables?" This question, deriving from a popular phrase they most likely know well, gets students thinking about the absorption of nutrients, the primary aim of digestion.

Delaying the prompt is based on an awareness that before adolescents can write successfully in response to a given prompt they need time and practice thinking and learning (i.e., writing to learn) about the topic. Activities encouraging students to explore and get to know the topic on their own align with the concept of getting to know their own beliefs about a topic—a central component of theory of mind.

- *Making Predictions.* "What do you think will happen next?" "How will the earth system change in the future?" "What would happen if you went back in time and accidently killed your grandfather?" "If [fill in the blank] is faced with (a) imprisonment or (b) giving up his/her beliefs, what will he/she choose?" These are sample questions asking adolescent writers to make predictions.

Making predictions is a generative imaginary space wherein adolescent writers form inferences based on what they already know to make predictions about what they think will happen. Since making predictions necessitates viewing imaginary scenarios from the perspective of others and oneself, this is an ideal writing-to-learn activity facilitating thinking associated with theory of mind.

- *Theorizing Others.* This strategy hones in on theory of mind processing by asking adolescents to theorize the thoughts of others. There are several activities that accomplish this.

Ask adolescents to imagine the thoughts of others within photographs. I recently did this in my own classroom. I projected five images of people engaged in daily activities. These were candid pictures. For each image I had my students write for four minutes the internal dialogue of the people. Students engaged with this activity quickly and had no difficulties writing the thoughts of those projected on the screen—indeed, we are hardwired to immediately try to read the thoughts of others.

This activity is easily customized for different disciplines. For example, in a mathematics problem you can present someone pondering the fastest route to a desired destination. In a social studies classroom you can project the image of a historical figure and ask students to think through an obstacle the person faced.

Class readings also provide wonderful departure points. Ask students to extend the thoughts of characters in the reading (this activity works equally well with fiction and nonfiction texts). What question, for example, would they most want to ask a character and how would that character respond? What are a certain character's motivations? Fears? Any number of questions can be posed in which adolescent writers practice stepping into the minds of characters they are reading about and theorize their thoughts and corresponding actions.

Class can also provide an opening to adopt a new point of view. Ask students to retell part of a reading from another point of view—perhaps from the point of view of a minor or less privileged character or historical figure.

We're all expert people watchers. Whether sitting in a park, riding in subway, walking down a crowded sidewalk—invariably someone catches your attention and you begin to imagine the life that person leads. Why does she walk quickly? What is that man in the red hat thinking? Why is that child sitting by herself? We are persistent mind readers. Theory of mind tells us this is an evolved trait and that imagining the thoughts of others gives us information about the social world around us, information that can be useful when negotiating with others and considering our own place in the social world.

Ask students to walk around the school or neighborhood practicing their mind-reading, people-watching skills. This makes for an engaging homework assignment. What do they theorize about the lives of others around them? What are they basing their theories on? Writing in response to such an activity helps students refine their powers of observation and persuasion as they uncover the observable "facts" to support claims about these imagined lives.

WRITING-TO-SHOW-LEARNING: THEORIZING OTHERS IN THE WRITING PROCESS

- *Grocery List.* This is a quick and highly effective technique for helping adolescent writers understand the value and necessity of considering outside readers while writing. First, have students jot down a list of items they would get if going to the grocery store. What would they buy?

After sharing out an item or two from their list have students revise their list if someone else were going to do their shopping for them. If they were to give their list to a family member or friend to do their shopping for them how would they revise their list? Have students share their revised lists by reading an original item and then the revised description of the item to purchase.

The final step is to have students think about and answer the following questions: How did you revise your list? What are the differences between the list written for yourself and the list written for someone else? What was your strategy when revising?

This discussion underscores the ways they rewrote based on moving from a list written for themselves to a list written for another person. For example, "milk" becomes "half-gallon 2% from the back of the cooler, not the front" and "cereal" becomes "one box of Special K with red berries." The role audience conceptualization plays in the writing process becomes immediately apparent.

- *Read aloud.* Another quick and easy activity with positive implications for audience awareness is to simply ask students to read their writing aloud. The act of reading aloud evokes an audience and students invariably begin to identify points of confusion and grammatical missteps that were not visible when the writing was confined to their headspace alone.

Here is what one adolescent writer had to say about this activity: "I think reading our work out loud helps us see errors and what needs work easier than when we read it in our heads. It is easier to miss things when we read our writing silently."

- *Questions for Peers.* This activity works by having adolescent writers formulate questions about their writing to ask peers. Questions such as "What do you know about my topic already?" and "What are you interested in learning about my topic?" help to reinforce the concept of peers as audience. Adolescent writers can also be encouraged to ask such questions of other potential audiences such as family members and acquaintances.
- *Procedural Writing.* This can be an amusing activity that works especially well in math and science classrooms where order of operations is of primary concern. A popular version of procedural writing is to have students write out directions for how to make a peanut butter–and-jelly sandwich. After they are done with their directions the teacher can follow the directions at the front of the room.

    Directions such as "put the peanut butter on the bread" can be interpreted by the teacher placing the jar of peanut butter on the bread and "spread the jam over the peanut butter" can be interpreted by spreading the jam over the jar of peanut butter or—for the adventurous—using one's fingers to spread the jam since the use of the butter knife was omitted. This exercise dramatically and humorously imparts the value of paying attention to detail and the importance of avoiding ambiguous sentences while conceptualizing outside audience.
- *Counterclaim.* Invaluable to persuasive writing assignments, counterclaim refers to the rhetorical strategy of anticipating and rebutting the counterarguments to one's claim. A strong counterclaim demonstrates an ability to view one's claim from not only another perspective, but the perspective of readers who are most apt to disagree with one's own position. Adding such refutation to writing assignments helps adolescent writers create more responsive, robust persuasive arguments that are multidimensional and nuanced in their positions.

- *Peer Review.* If only a single writing strategy could be integrated into adolescent classrooms across content areas for greatest effect, this is it. Peer review is the single most important writing activity I've come across in my years of teaching writing. Peer review belongs in this chapter on theory of mind because peer review is all about confronting an actual audience of one's peers.

Educators who have integrated peer review into their teaching fall generally into two camps: those that absolutely love the process and those that think it's a colossal waste of time. When I talk to adolescents about their experiences with peer review I get the same reaction as the educators: Peer review has a tendency to work well or not at all. My answer for this dilemma is peer review needs scaffolding to work effectively. (Much of what follows about peer review is adapted from *Writing Classrooms Live and Die by the Quality of Peer Review* [Wirtz, 2012].)

There are three major ways to structure peer review—author in the group, author outside the group, and individual exchange. Each of these has its advantages, and generally I work through each in a sequential manner because of how they situate the writer and the type of response he or she receives. Here is a quick explanation of each type of peer review:

1. *Author in the group.* The author reads aloud his or her paper or the students can rotate the papers. If the author is going to read his or her paper out loud, it's best if they bring three to four copies so that group members can see as well as hear the paper.
2. *Author outside the group.* Groups gather their papers and exchange with another group. Generally, the level of critique rises when the author is not in the group because students have an easier time being critical when the author is not sitting across from them.
3. *Individual exchange.* This is a very focused peer review in which students individually exchange papers with one another for commentary. The students work independently and then meet to discuss the feedback. This places a great deal of onus on each student to provide in-depth commentary because they do not have the benefit of working within a collective group.

Here are some strategies to facilitate the process across all three types of peer review:

1. *Students identify their concerns.* This is a first and necessary step for all peer review sessions. Have students write out three to five concerns they have with their paper. Then ask students to share these con-

cerns while keeping a running list of these concerns on the chalk/whiteboard.

This list of concerns helps reviewers focus their comments. This list of concerns also helps the reviewers be more critical since this is feedback that the author has asked for. The master list of concerns on the chalk/whiteboard also helps the teacher to informally assess what students are having difficulty with in relation to the assignment. The master list also becomes a place to clarify concepts.

For example, if a student mentions "flow" as a concern, press them to explain what they mean by flow. This process of defining terms helps to create a shared discourse that becomes the backbone of clear communication during peer review. Finally, this master list becomes a generative place for peer-review groups to look when they feel they have exhausted their critiques.

2. *Students articulate the changes they made based on peer-review feedback and the feedback they provided to their peers.* These are two paragraphs students should write at the end of every major writing assignment that is turned in for teacher commentary. The first paragraph asks the author to speak to the peer-review process in terms of the feedback they received. What were the peer suggestions? How were these suggestions incorporated into the revision process? What feedback was not incorporated and why?

The second paragraph asks the author to reflect on the feedback provided for peers—the more concrete and specific the better. I generally ask for at least three specific examples. These two paragraphs not only help to assess the quality of the peer-review sessions but help to facilitate the peer-review sessions as well.

For example, I can read over these comments and get a good sense as to how the peer-review sessions are working, or not working, for students. I can make a list of comments that I want to talk over with the whole class, comments that are valued because they are straight from the students themselves.

These two paragraphs also facilitate the peer-review process because I am armed with the language of: "Remember, you need to write a paragraph based on the changes you've made to your essay as a result of peer review. This means you have to offer your peers critical feedback that will help to improve their essay and to write this paragraph." These two paragraphs oftentimes become the much-needed excuse students need to be usefully critical with one another.

3. *Exit slips.* I have students complete exit slips on most peer-review days. Here are a few examples from my class this week: "Based on peer review I will add more citations. I find this process useful and hope to do it in the future." This tells me a great deal about this student since this student had to be told to put away her German homework and a few times I thought she was going to fall asleep. I've had lively e-mails from her in the past that demonstrate her engagement in the class but her classroom affect is the opposite—she looks withdrawn. This comment helps me to theorize/understand that perhaps this student is engaged even though she doesn't show it.

Another example: "Peer Review: I should focus on other resources and write down my own ideas rather than quote from the resources." This is an ESL student who is having difficulty keeping up with her native-speaking counterparts. This exit slip was heartening for me because I fear that her research paper will contain an overreliance on the sources. I'm glad that she's getting this information from her peers.

Another example: "Peer review was a great opportunity to receive criticism that I wouldn't have seen. The review helps refine our papers." This is a positive response with, really, no depth. This is most likely a stock answer—what this student thinks I want to hear.

Contrast that exit slip with another: "Peer review was helpful. It helped me to see what other literary techniques/styles are effective. Also helped me to identify strengths, and what should be left alone. My issue of sticking to my thesis was resolved." Much more content here—specific, identifiable results from the peer-review session, which demonstrates in a concrete manner the progress that this student was able to make.

Peer review has such potential that it should be incorporated in any classroom focused on improving the writing of adolescents. To conclude, here is a quote from an adolescent summarizing her experiences after being in a classroom that utilized peer review as a foundational strategy for writing development:

The consistent peer reviewing that we engaged in helped me to realize the use of, and learn how to use, criticism. I have always had trouble using criticism gained during peer review. I have often ignored the suggestions of my peers, wondering what gave them the authority to say how my work could be improved. In this class, however, we engaged in multiple peer reviews with various partners. When more than one of my peer reviewers mentioned similar things, I felt far more inclined to listen to those suggestions. On the whole, I learned how to sort through feedback and synthesize the suggestions that I think are the most helpful and important into my work.

BRINGING IT ALL TOGETHER: PERSONAL NARRATIVE WRITING AND THEORY OF MIND

The genre of personal narrative is ideal for bringing together writing to learn (audience as self) and writing to show learning (audience as other). Personal narrative necessitates learning about oneself based on experiential reflection and then communicating what one has learned with an outside audience. It is a demand of the genre to weave introspection with communication.

While personal narrative assignments come in a variety of shapes and sizes I will share one specific assignment called "In the Moment." As a precursor to the assignment description, I present here an excerpt from a student paper. The title of this student's personal narrative is "The Last Time I Took the 21 Bus" and the narrative revolves and evolves around viewing a case of domestic violence on a public bus. These are the final two paragraphs:

> As the bus shuddered to a stop, the one who'd been crying pitched over and nearly fell onto me. Up close, I could see that she was shockingly young and gaunt. Her skin, though splotched and pale, was smooth as a child's. Her eyes were empty, though, as if by refusing to see she could refuse to grant her experiences any room in her psyche. I didn't want to look at her. I didn't want her to see me in my new wool coat, snuggled into the arms of my sweet boyfriend. I tried to summon up every bit of compassion I could into a smile. *I don't know how to help you!* The smile was meant to say. *I don't know why you're so broken, and I wouldn't have the slightest idea how to fix you. But I'm on your side, for what it's worth!*
>
> The girl steadied herself against my seat. She took one look at my foolish beaming, rolled her eyes, and stalked off down the aisle and out the door.

There are several connections to theory of mind in this exemplary student excerpt. The passage begins with the author looking to provide compassion for the girl whom she theorizes as being in trouble. The author has read the body language of the girl and has decided that she is in need of emotional support as noted in the line: "Her eyes were empty, though, as if by refusing to see she could refuse to grant her experiences any room in her psyche."

The author then decides to offer emotional support but not in an obvious manner since her "wool coat" and "sweet boyfriend" are too brute a contrast, potentially making her efforts look condescending. In this scene the author demonstrates a remarkable ability to theorize herself through the eyes of the troubled girl.

The last paragraph is the most significant as the author pulls the rug from underneath our feet, defying reader expectations as well as her own as the troubled girl shoots back a look of disdain in response to her "foolish beaming."

This excerpt is a strong example of a writer demonstrating felicity with theory of mind as she weaves in and out of her own thinking, the theoretical thoughts of the character about whom she writes, and finally the expectations and experience of her readers.

The following are some of the instructions provided to students when writing their "In the Moment" personal narratives:

- Place your readers into a significant moment you've experienced. Narrow your focus from the start. Select a narrative out of one tiny, narrow corner of your life and avoid expanding on all the details around the story.
- Do not give your readers an introduction explaining everything before it happens. Let the narrative speak for itself and trust your readers to work at discovering what your narrative is about. Drop your readers into the narrative immediately to create immediacy.
- Context should be embedded into the narrative, not provided as a separate section. Pay particular attention to character development by asking yourself what actions best represent the people included in your narrative.
- Relate your narrative in a way that reveals its significance to you. If the narrative is revealing to you as you write then your readers will experience it as a revelation. Don't simply write about the event, show us how you experienced it as opposed to what it means to you or what you learned from the experience. This is very tricky to pull off successfully. On the one hand, you don't want to over-tell the narrative in such a way that gives your readers nothing to make sense of on their own. On the other hand, you don't want to alienate your readers by confusing them with not enough information to see and comprehend your moment.
- Use concrete and specific detail to represent your point of view and your moment. Avoid direct explanation in favor of concrete details that show the reader what you mean, rather than tell the reader. Attach your ideas to visible things. In general, you want to dramatize your moment so that your readers experience it as though it were happening before their eyes, so readers are in the position of an observer at the scene.
- Avoid explanatory epilogue conclusions summing up everything for your readers. Trust your readers to draw their own conclusions from the moment you've crafted for them to experience.

THEORY OF MIND AND WRITING:
CONNECTIONS TO THE ENGLISH LANGUAGE
ARTS WRITING COMMON CORE STATE STANDARDS

Across the board, and the CCSS are no exception, standards are to request Writing to Show Learning. The Writing to Learn activities in this chapter are then best viewed as invaluable primers and explorations that lead toward the type of finished writing privileged by the CCSS and other standards for writing.

The *Procedural Writing* strategy in this chapter meets the CCSS of "Write informative/explanatory texts, including the narration of historical events, scientific procedures/experiments, or technical processes" (CCSS. ELA-Literacy.WHST.11-12.2). Additionally, the *Counterclaim* strategy provided is most relevant since "counterclaims" is noted several times within the CCSS.

The strategy with the strongest overt connections to the CCSS is *Peer Review*. This strategy meets all the CCSS listed under "Production and Distribution of Writing":

- "Produce clear and coherent writing in which the development, organization, and style are appropriate to task, purpose, and audience." (CCSS.ELA-Literacy.WHST.11-12.4)
- "Develop and strengthen writing as needed by planning, revising, editing, rewriting, or trying a new approach, focusing on addressing what is most significant for a specific purpose and audience." (CCSS. ELA-Literacy.WHST.11-12.5)
- "Use technology, including the internet, to produce, publish, and update individual or shared writing products in response to ongoing feedback, including new arguments or information." (CCSS.ELA-Literacy.WHST.11-12.6)

Because *Peer Review* places such emphasis on audience and the integration of feedback, it is essential to meeting the CCSS.

Personal Narrative writing as described in this chapter meets the CCSS call for narrative skills: "Write narratives to develop real or imagined experiences or events using effective technique, well-chosen details, and well-structured event sequences" (CCSS.ELA-Literacy.W.11-12.3). The "In the Moment" assignment descried in this chapter meets all of the standards associated with narrative in the CCSS.

WHERE WE'VE BEEN AND WHERE WE'RE GOING

This chapter explains theory of mind from the perspective of brain science and the perspective of writer-teachers. The activities offered are crafted to position adolescent writers to use writing as a tool for their own learning (writing to learn) and communication with others (writing to show learning). The concept of audience is central in this chapter. Writers at all levels are empowered when they can invoke various audiences at different stages of the writing process.

The next chapter, *Brain States and Writing*, introduces and illustrates the concept of brain states and its relevance to the writing process. Several activities linking brain states to writing instruction are presented and detailed.

3

✛

Brain States and Writing

INTRODUCTION AND CHAPTER OVERVIEW

We endlessly weave in and out of varying brain states. We are in different brain states, for example, when awake as opposed to when we are asleep, or when we are at work as opposed to socializing with friends. Other easily identifiable brain states accompany hunger or fear, and as a dramatic example, we are clearly in a different brain state under anesthesia.

This chapter explains the concept of brain states from the scientific perspective as well as the perspective of writer-teachers. Several connections between brain states and teaching writing to adolescent learners are presented and described.

THE SCIENTIFIC VIEW OF BRAIN STATES

A helpful metaphor to illustrate the concept of brain states comes from neuroscientist Robert Stickgold, who compares brain states to different software programs run on a computer: "Neuromodulators shift us into different brain states like the same computer using different software" (2014). In this metaphor the hardware is the brain and the software is the various brain states available.

Another example from the sciences illustrating the prevalence of brain states is the distinction made between the default mode network and the cognitive control network. In brief, the default mode network is the brain state of daydreaming and mind wandering whereas the cognitive control network is the brain state associated with focused attention on a given cognitive task.

There are two corresponding ideas to note about brain states. First, the concept of brain states helps elucidate a central principal of brain science: the significance of integrated networks in the brain, or what is often called connectionism. Brain science has a long history of debate between those holding to localization of brain function (i.e., specific areas of the brain carrying out specific functions) and those holding to holistic approaches to brain function (i.e., many or all parts of the brain being involved in cognitive functions). We now know that both views are in part correct.

While certain lower-level functions can be localized to specific areas of the brain (but not specific neurons), higher-level functions such as writing exist as interconnected networks across the brain. Because writing is such a complex cognitive skill there is no single location in the brain that houses our ability to write. This has important educational implications since to teach writing is to engage several different cognitive networks, or brain states.

A second important finding from brain science is that there are indeed brain states that are more or less conducive to learning. While educators have implicitly or experientially understood that certain brain states can enhance or depress learning, evidence from the sciences helps to confirm such understanding.

Research in brain science demonstrates that certain brain states can serve as predictors of performance in a variety of perceptual, memory, and problem-solving tasks. For example, a study out of MIT and Harvard (Yoo et al., 2012) used real-time fMRI to accurately predict performance on a memory task. In this study subjects were placed in an fMRI scanner and shown indoor and outdoor scenes, which were to be studied for a subsequent recall test.

The images were displayed to the study subjects when they were either in a "good" or "bad" brain state for learning. The real-time fMRI data detected what was a "good" or "bad" brain state by monitoring activity in the parahippocampal cortex (PHC), an area of the brain known to be essential for memory formation of scenes.

The recall test showed that study subjects were better at remembering those scenes presented in a "good" brain state and worse at remembering those scenes presented in a "bad" brain state. These findings demonstrate an ability to identify "good" and "bad" states for learning in the brain.

Once again the news from brain science is encouraging as it reinforces what have long been held as good teaching practices. The fact that different brain states are more conducive to learning provides traction for classroom time devoted to creating a positive learning environment. Time spent motivating learning, building classroom culture, and orchestrating

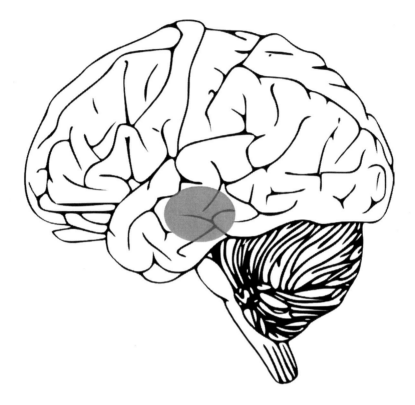

Figure 3.1. Location of the parahippocampal cortex (PHC), an area of the brain known to be essential for memory formation of scenes.

anticipatory learning experiences can no longer be viewed as peripheral to instruction.

WRITER-TEACHERS SPEAK TO BRAIN STATES

The concept of brain states surfaces quickly when speaking with writer-teachers as they consistently reference the importance of cultivating a brain state conducive to the writing process. Elizabeth Nunez shares her process of achieving a brain state optimal for writing:

It's a dream state that you're creating. I always say my house is cleanest when I'm writing because I have to do something physical and get the satisfaction that there's some completion. So if I wash the dishes, I'm doing something physical and I can see that the dishes are clean, or I can see that the laundry is done. And all the time I'm doing that I'm thinking, I'm working out the novel. But eventually in that state I will find the state [of mind].

Deborah Brandt speaks to the brain state for writing as an intense focus, noting the difficulty of working oneself into such a state:

> It's intense focus and you want to keep your focus and it takes me sometimes a while to get back into something if I've been writing the day before. It will take me an hour just to warm myself back up to where I was and the frame of mind I was in. I don't make outlines; I will often have notes to the side about what's coming up. I don't know what that's about but it is, there's a lot of focus there, that's what I mean when I say writing is a state of being.

As we get a sense of what this brain state for writing feels like experientially, a related line of inquiry takes shape around how writers enter into and maintain a brain state for writing.

Writing habits and rituals serve as neuromodulators to help writers maintain a brain state most conducive to writing. This point is easily made with famous examples in the extreme such as James Joyce donning a white coat while writing, Ernest Hemingway always standing before his writing board, and Friedrich Schiller keeping a drawer of rotting fruit in his writing desk. While there is nothing a white coat, standing, or a drawer of rotting fruit can do for another writer, the important takeaway is that writers utilize such rituals and habits to serve as neuromodulators to help transition into and maintain a brain state conducive to writing.

Common habits and rituals around writing that surface across interviews with writer-teachers include running/walking while thinking about a writing project and the importance of choosing carefully one's instruments for writing. As representative examples, here is Art Markman talking about the value of walking his dog before writing, followed by Deborah Brandt speaking to the importance of pens with a thick line:

> Art Markman: So I spent a lot of time—I have a dog, so when I walk the dog people think I'm boring because I take the same route with the dog every time. The dog doesn't seem to mind and if I don't have to pay attention to where I'm going I can think about something else and I'll spend a lot of time thinking about whatever chapter I'm working on so I usually have that pretty well mapped out. I'll get back after a walk and make a couple of notes to myself and e-mail that to myself but then have that altogether so that when I actually sit down to write I'm more putting words to ideas I've already been thinking about rather than trying to come up with what in the world I'm going to write about while I'm sitting there.

Deborah Brandt: For my journals the pen has to have a thick line. It makes my handwriting look better so some pens make my handwriting look worse and I don't like it.

Another essential habit, or neuromodulator, is the atmosphere writer-teachers construct around themselves as they work. This careful attention to time and place and overall environment is shared across the interviewees.

Leora Tanenbaum, for example, chooses to work in a place called "The Writer's Room." As she describes it: "It's just a big loft carved up into cubicles, and you pay an annual fee, and it's first-come, first-serve in terms of which cubicle you get every day. You just go, and you bring your laptop or whatever you're using, and you can just sit there all day and work." This space was necessary for her writing because, as she explains, "Being at home is just like a pit of procrastination, and there are very legitimate, valid things that I could be doing at any time so being away from home is really important for me." All the writer-teachers interviewed are deliberate about creating an environment most suitable for writing.

The final insight to share from interviews with writer-teachers is different parts of the writing process demand different brain states. James Gee describes the way in which he parses out his writing time to reflect this understanding: "I tend to write in the morning and I'll spend two to three hours writing every morning. That's when I'm most productive and I kind of separate what I do between writing where I'm admitting new material, kind of the first-draft type stuff versus where I'm revising what I've already written and I will tend to do that more in the afternoon when I've got less energy. I see those two processes as different. One is coming up with new material and one is chiseling and perfecting and they're two different tasks and I view them as different things. I enjoy both of them but I tend to separate them."

This insight has implications for the teaching of writing as will be taken up in the next section. The fact that different brain states are required of different stages of the writing process means we must assist adolescent writers in developing these various habits of mind.

BRAIN STATES AND TEACHING WRITING

There are three areas where the concept of brain states can readily transition to writing pedagogy.

1. Adolescent writers need encouragement personalizing their habits, tools, and environments for writing.
2. Adolescent writers need practice transitioning in and out of the brain states required of writing. Because writing is a complex cognitive skill a number of brain states—even those that conflict—must be called upon at various times within the process.
3. An invaluable tool—academic language—must be explicitly emphasized in any classroom focused on writing instruction. Academic language is a tool through which adolescent writers cultivate brain states appropriate to the discipline in which they are writing.

Habits, Tools, and Environment: Encouraging Adolescent Writers to Personalize Their Approaches to Writing

I enjoy asking adolescent writers about their writing habits and I'm consistently surprised by the variety of responses. I've heard about writing pillows, specific musical tastes while writing, even the importance of lighting—one student turns off all the lights in her room, puts on sunglasses, and then writes at her computer with the brightness setting on high.

A strategy to get adolescent writers thinking about their own habits, tools, and environments when writing is to have them respond to the prompt: "Describe your ideal environment for writing." A few scaffolding questions include:

- Do you prefer writing in the morning or evening?
- Can you write with the television on? In a crowded place? Do you prefer silence?
- If you write with music, what kind? Does it matter if there are lyrics or do you prefer it be primarily instrumentals?
- What kind of food or drink do you like to have, or not have, around you when writing?
- What role do deadlines play in your writing process?
- Do you prefer being alone when writing or is it ok to have other people around you?

One of the advantages afforded adolescent learners is they are very much in the process of cultivating their writing habits, rituals, and ideal environments. With this in mind, it becomes useful to have them experiment with different routines.

- Adopt a Strategy. In this activity adolescent writers experiment with different writing routines by trying out what a peer may be doing. After polling the class and discussing the various habits and strategies used across the entire class (a master list can be generated), adolescent writers identify a couple of writing strategies they plan to try on, strategies that differ from their own but work for their peers. This activity works well in large part because adolescent writers are generally keen to adopt a strategy utilized by a peer and report back on the experience.
- Responding to deadlines is another place to encourage adolescent writers to make modifications. Rather than being driven by external deadlines adolescent writers should set their own, working up to the completion of a writing assignment by their own measured progress.
- Setting Mini-Deadlines. In this activity adolescent writers are asked to set their own mini-deadlines for a writing assignment, keeping in mind the externally appointed deadline. This activity requires them to consider their own writing process, the time they have available for writing, and the division of the writing assignment into smaller, workable units that can be completed. Have students use a calendar to create mini-deadlines in service to the final deadline. These mini-deadlines ensure that the final, external deadline is met. As a bonus, this activity squarely reinforces time-management skills.

We know that binge writers do not produce the quantity or quality of consistent writers. Writing in consistent, smaller increments is smarter than writing for a long period in one sitting because a deadline is fast approaching. Being cognizant of successful writing habits makes for better writing and writers.

From Receptivity to Discernment: Different Parts of the Writing Process Call for Different Brain States

We learn from coordinating knowledge from the brain sciences and interviews with writer-teachers that writing is a complex skill set requiring an interweaving of varying brain states. At minimum, adolescent writers will need to learn how to approach brain states favorable to stages of invention, drafting, feedback, revision, and editing. Perhaps most important is the foundational knowledge from writing studies that writing is a recursive, iterative process. As a result, these stages in the writing process with accompanying states of mind must be seen as being in conversation and negotiation with one another.

Each of these stages of the writing process will be explored along a spectrum of brain states from receptivity to discernment. Receptivity represents the most open brain state for writing in which the writer is inclusively considering ideas, searching for possibilities, wanting to be surprised by what the writing process reveals. The widest net is cast within this brain state of receptivity as no idea is considered too outrageous.

Discernment is the brain state at the other end of the spectrum in which the writer is now making solid decisions about what should and should not be included. Discernment is a brain state for refining the writing and making final decisions about its content and organization. Figure 3.2 helps illustrate this spectrum between receptivity and discernment, noting where several stages of the writing process most often fall along this spectrum.

RECEPTIVITY   DISCERNMENT

Invention - Drafting - Feedback - Revising - Editing

Figure 3.2.

- *Invention.* One of Aristotle's five canons of rhetoric, invention refers to the search for what to write about—the ideas and concepts to be explored or thesis to be argued, supported, and defended. The brain state associated with invention is one of openness. Writing-to-learn strategies are most appropriate here such as freewriting and open-ended exploration of topic ideas. Along the spectrum from receptivity to discernment, invention is most closely allied with receptivity as the writer is positioned to discover one's topic and write one's way into further understanding.
- *Drafting.* The drafting stage is earmarked by quantity over quality. Getting the words on the page/screen is most important, knowing revisions will come later in the process. The most common misstep in this process is to begin refining or editing at the same time as drafting. As drafting and editing brain states are at odds with one another, this can potentially limit and even paralyze the writer.
- *Feedback.* This is a potentially difficult brain state for adolescent writers to inhabit because they have not often been asked to do this type of thinking wherein they have discerned their topic and written a draft but must then suspend their own beliefs about the writing to be receptive to critique from readers. Feedback is where discernment (knowing what you are writing about) and receptivity (being open to the views of an outside audience) are most apt to conflict. Adoles-

cent writers need prompting and practice navigating between these two brain states in order to integrate feedback successfully into their writing.

- *Revising.* Getting closer to the discernment end of the spectrum, revision is a brain state marked by (a) knowing what needs to be changed within the writing and (b) executing a plan for revisions. The most common mistake at this stage is writers not treating revision in a significant manner, not actually carrying out a "re-vision" of the work. It's much easier to conflate revision with editing for local changes such as spelling and grammar since it's easier to inhabit a brain state of discernment than be receptive to conceptual changes when revising.
- *Editing.* The icing on the cake, editing is the final stage of the writing process in which all the major decisions have been made and now it's time to polish its final form. This stage of the writing process is most clearly marked by discernment over receptivity.
- *Writing Is an Iterative, Recursive Process:* The spectrum from receptivity to discernment is best conceptualized as a generative tension. This generative tension has deep roots that can be found in such paradoxical pairings as creator/editor, Apollonian/Dionysian, form/ freedom, and discovery/presentation.

A mark of the mature writer is the ability to bring these competing brain states into close proximity to service the writing. Returning to the interview data with accomplished teacher-writers, Diane Seuss speaks to this generative tension invoking her own pairing of mystical and analytical brain states:

> It sounds very mystical and partly it is, but partly it's really logical too. I think that's what's cool about it, two parts of the brain working in tandem. The formal stuff, what I'm thinking about line, what I'm thinking about music, that's nice and distracting and that allows the other stuff to kind of rise. I think it's a dual process, it's two tracks at once, and that is it's both mystical and really analytical and that's why the attention is so keen, that's why it's such a nice feeling, because everything is working together when you're cooking.

Having these "two parts of the brain working in tandem" is to take full advantage of the brain states of receptivity and discernment and promote successful transfer from one brain state to another. Successful transfer is what makes the generative tension between receptivity and discernment productive for the writer.

How do we help adolescent writers cultivate this ability to transfer? One way is to have them think about and respond to questions about such transfer. Questions to encourage the articulation of transfer between writing stages and their accompanying brain states include:

- Tell the story of how your invention process eventually led you to your final written product. How did you come up with your ideas for the writing? Were there any surprises along the way?
- How did you incorporate the feedback you received into your revisions?
- Was there a time when you had to revisit earlier stages in the writing process such as invention or revision when you thought you were ready for the final, editing stage?
- The writing process rarely works in strict chronological fashion from invention → drafting→ feedback → revising → editing. Describe your own process. How did you dip in and out of these stages along the way? Describe a time when you had to return to a previous stage in the writing process.

Encouraging adolescent writers to recognize their own organic, circuitous, iterative process and to personalize their own approaches reinforces the understanding that writing is not a chronological process leading to a "correct" response in the way that many standardized test items, for example, are structured. Writing requires a complex array of interweaving brain states inhabited at different times for different purposes. Most important, the mature writer purposefully facilitates successful transfer between these brain states.

Academic Language: Developing Disciplinary Thinking

Academic language references two complementary uses of language. First academic language refers to language that is more academic than interpersonal, more school based than social. Second, academic language is the utilization of disciplinary-specific language. The term "proof," for example, holds particular meaning depending upon the discipline in which it is being employed. "Proof" means something different in the discipline of English than it does in mathematics.

The argument behind explicitly teaching academic language is that the writer cannot participate in a discipline without understanding the language of that discipline. This interview excerpt from the poet William Olsen helps illustrate the centrality of language within a given discipline:

In the morning my mind is a tabula rasa, it's a blackboard without any words written on it, and for me to enter the linguistic realm, the creative realm of poetry, I have to hear the language, I have to find my way into that language and not only that, find my way into a language built around perceptual activity as opposed to informational activity like a newspaper or even strictly intellectual activity.

This experience of finding one's "way into language" is not unique to the poet. It can be argued that disciplines themselves are structured around the language that typifies them. Finding one's way into the appropriate language of a discipline is synonymous with finding one's way into the brain state of the discipline.

In our classrooms we want our adolescent learners not to learn about biology and history for the sake of regurgitating on a test, but rather to think and write like biologists and historians, to see the world from the perspective, the brain state, of the biologist and historian. Academic language is the primary tool to stimulate disciplinary perception.

- *Making Academic Language Explicit.* All too often academic language remains an implicit expectation in the writing classroom and therefore invisible to students. An effective way to raise awareness is by showing examples where one passage takes further advantage of academic language than another. In table 3.1, read the following two introductions to a research paper. Which is more academic? What are the indicators that help you reach this conclusion?

Table 3.1.

Passage A	Passage B
Hospital Emergency Preparedness	Hospital Emergency Preparedness
"By failing to prepare, you are preparing to fail." As articulated by notable intellectual and founding father Benjamin Franklin, a lack of resources coupled with minimal preparation can result in an inability to confront and withstand potential calamities. Medical centers are often on the front-line when the negative consequences of external events such as floods, fires, and other natural disasters arise. Based on interviews conducted with several experienced and knowledgeable professionals on issues of emergency preparedness in hospitals, my goal is to understand how urban medical centers plan and prepare for an array of serious dangers.	"By failing to prepare, you are preparing to fail." This is a quote by Benjamin Franklin, an important man and founding father of the United States of America. His point was that a lack of resources and preparation will result in a loss of one's ability to live through different disasters. Medical centers are usually the first to have to deal with natural disasters such as floods, fires, and other natural disasters. I interviewed people at hospitals who work on emergency preparedness to find out how hospitals plan to deal with natural disasters when they arise. This research paper is about what I learned concerning how urban medical centers plan for these serious dangers.

Overall, Passage A employs more academic language than Passage B. Here are some of the academic language indicators to point out to adolescent writers:

- An important indicator of academic language is sentence complexity. While Passage B actually has more words than Passage A, Passage A has longer, more complex compound sentences (three sentences + the opening quote) than Passage B (five sentences + the opening quote).
- Passage A has less vague language. Examples of vague language from passage B include "an important man," "his point was that," and "this research paper is about."
- While personal pronouns such as "I" and "my" are not eliminated altogether in Passage A, they are minimized in favor of bolder claims standing on their own merit.
- Passage A has less unnecessary repetition. For example, the term "natural disasters" is repeated in Passage B for no added effect.

A final point is that academic language exists along a spectrum. Passage B has plenty of academic language and is quite clear in its communication. Passage B is in fact quite successful in many of its uses of academic language. Passage A, however, has more indicators of academic language in comparison to Passage B.

Academic Language Scavenger Hunt

Another strategy to surface and thus make explicit the academic language particular to disciplines such as biology, history, dance, or mathematics is to conduct an academic language scavenger hunt. In this activity adolescent writers, working individually or in pairs or small groups, look for the "buzz" words of a particular discipline.

In a biology classroom, for example, students can be asked to look for language that biologists use. If you were to interview someone to see what they knew about biology, to find out if they were a true biologist, what questions would you ask and what key words would you look for in their answers?

A great resource for the language scavenger hunt activity is the classroom textbook. What words are privileged in the textbook? Other great resources include journal articles in the field or more popular informational articles or videos trying to reach a wider audience within a given discipline. Making explicit the academic language of a discipline helps adolescent writers not only become more aware of academic language but facilitates the transfer of this language into their own writing.

Entering the Conversation

This strategy focuses on transferring disciplinary language into one's writing. In this strategy adolescent writers are given any number of reading selections privileging the academic language of a discipline. The adolescents are asked to circle the academic language terms and phrases and review the meanings and definitions of these terms before writing their own piece in which these terms and phrases are utilized. The goal of this activity is to have adolescent writers learn that a shared sense of language sets the stage to enter into a conversation.

Using the Academic Language of Another

There are four ways of integrating the language of another person into one's own writing: the direct quotation, long or block quotation, paraphrase, and the embedded quotation.

The direct quotation is just as it sounds—the writer offers up a quotation directly from the reading. For example: Usha Goswami argues that "Brain volume quadruples between birth and adulthood, because of the proliferation of connections, not because of the production of new neurons" (36). The long or block quotation works in much the same way except the quotation is usually three sentences or more in length.

Paraphrase and the embedded quotation I always introduce to adolescent writers as the more challenging. Adolescents often respond to this challenge by wanting to prove they can use these two types of quotations. The paraphrase takes the content of the quotation and presents it in the author's own words, still citing the original source. For example: As the brain grows from birth to adulthood it becomes as much as four times its original size because of all the new connections it develops (Goswami, 36).

The embedded quotation is perhaps the most difficult of them all. The embedded quotation weaves the voice of the writer within the quotation. For example: The importance of connections within the brain cannot be overemphasized as "brain volume quadruples between birth and adulthood, because of the proliferation of connections" (Goswami, 36).

- *The Sandwich Technique* is a strategy to help adolescent writers think about how they present quotations within their writing. In this technique the top piece of bread on the sandwich introduces the quotation, the meat (or whatever you put in your sandwiches) is the quotation itself, and the bottom piece of bread explains to the reader how the quotation supports the writer's larger ideas. What follows is an exemplary example from an adolescent writer illustrating this technique:

Due to stereotypes that view girls as good readers and boys as good with mathematics, girls are encouraged toward humanities-based subjects such as history and English and steered away from science and math. They are pushed toward the humanities by their teachers and parents, who may believe they are simply encouraging their students and daughters to pursue what they are good at.

While the idea that males are analytically minded while females are linguistically minded is still the subject of much debate, *TIME* magazine in April of 2014 published an article revealing that over the span of the past ninety-seven years, from 1914 to 2011, elementary- and high school–age girls have consistently maintained higher grades than their male classmates in all subjects, including math and science (Park).

Whether this is indicative of natural ability, brain wiring, or study habits and work ethic is of little importance, what is significant about this study is that it is evidence that young girls can not only match but surpass young boys in math and science subjects. Female students not only can achieve adequate grades, they can excel in all their subjects.

The more explicit and specific we can be about these "insider" academic indicators the easier it becomes for adolescents to transfer them into their own writing. Try creating your own list of insider academic indicators for your discipline, academic indicators made explicit for the purpose of sharing with adolescent writers.

- *Ethos, Logos, and Pathos.* Contemporary academic writing borrows heavily from ancient rhetoric, which provides another place to look for pedagogical guides. Ethos, logos, and pathos are three different yet interrelated methods for couching academic arguments. An understanding of these three rhetorical appeals helps adolescent writers recognize and formulate effective arguments.

Ethos persuades the audience the person constructing the argument has credibility, or ethics. An example: "Based on fifteen years of teaching experience I can tell you it is important to be specific with students about how to construct sound arguments in their writing." Adolescents need to find ways of convincing their readers that they have the requisite understanding of their topic in order for their arguments to be considered.

An appeal to logic, logos persuades an audience through reason. An example: "More than one hundred peer-reviewed studies confirm the importance of low teacher-to-student ratios for educational success." Bringing to bear evidence in its many qualitative and quantitative forms in support of the writing is a necessary skill for adolescent learners when writing academic prose.

An appeal to emotion, pathos is a way of convincing an audience by creating an emotional response. An example: "Any credible view of the alleged decline of achievement in American schools would conclude that among the complex variables—cultural shifts, economic and social inequity, inadequate funding, poor public policy, lousy parenting—the only thing that has not changed is the dedication and skill of teachers."

Of the three, pathos is the rhetorical appeal least applied to academic writing. Effective pathos must be tempered to be effective in academic contexts and yet is an effective strategy demonstrating passion for the topic and resulting line of inquiry or argument.

- *Academic Discourse.* Keeping in mind the rich connections between talk and writing, it becomes invaluable to encourage adolescent use of academic discourse. Classrooms with opportunities for structured and semi-structured student-to-student and student-to-teacher discourse provide a platform for adolescents to practice academic language.

Structured discourse interactions include such activities as having adolescents teach one another or parrot back a learning concept to the teacher. Semi-structured interactions can be enabled by efficient pedagogical moves such as providing sufficient wait time to allow students to gather their thoughts before speaking or giving students time to write down their thoughts before sharing verbally. Other quick yet highly effective pedagogical moves include asking adolescents to incorporate a vocabulary term into their discourse or to rephrase a given response in a more academic manner.

The connection between academic learners employing the discourse of a discipline and the concept of brain states is a direct one: In utilizing the language of a discipline adolescents are participating in the brain state of that discipline, viewing the world from the disciplinary perspective of the English scholar, biologist, historian, mathematician, artist, etc.

BRAIN STATES AND WRITING: CONNECTIONS TO THE ENGLISH LANGUAGE ARTS WRITING COMMON CORE STATE STANDARDS

Academic language is central to the ELA Writing CCSS as evinced by phrases written into the standards such as: "discipline specific," "precise," "domain-specific," "expertise of likely readers," "a specific purpose and audience," and "specific task, purpose, and audience." This chapter meets the CCSS by providing strategies to develop academic language, including: *Making Academic Language Explicit, Academic Language Scavenger Hunt, Entering the Conversation,* and *Academic Discourse.* More specifically, these strategies directly meet the following standards:

- "Write arguments focused on *discipline-specific* content." (CCSS.ELA-Literacy.WHST.11-12.1)
- "Establish and maintain a formal style and objective tone while attending to the norms and conventions of the discipline in which they are writing." (CCSS.ELA-Literacy.WHST.11-12.1.D)
- "Use precise language, domain-specific vocabulary and techniques such as metaphor, simile, and analogy to manage the complexity of the topic; convey a knowledgeable stance in a style that responds to the discipline and context as well as to the expertise of likely readers." (CCSS. ELA-Literacy.WHST.11-12.2.D)

Using the Academic Language of Another is a strategy to teach adolescent writers different ways to incorporate evidence into their writing. This strategy meets the CCSS category of "Research to Build and Present Knowledge." Specifically, this strategy enables adolescent writers to "integrate information into the text selectively to maintain the flow of ideas, avoiding plagiarism and overreliance on any one source" (CCSS. ELA-Literacy.WHST.11-12.8) and "Draw evidence from informational texts to support analysis, reflection, and research" (CCSS.ELA-Literacy. WHST.11-12.9).

WHERE WE'VE BEEN AND WHERE WE'RE GOING

This chapter explains the concept of brain states from the perspective of brain science and teacher-writers. Strategies are offered to help adolescent writers personalize their writing habits and environments, draw from different brain states at different stages within a recursive writing process, and utilize academic language as a means to enter into and sustain disciplinary discourse.

The next chapter, *Brain Variation and Writing*, demonstrates the unique functionality of our brains from the standpoint of brain science research and writer-teacher experiences. Connections between brain variation and the teaching of writing will focus on differentiating instruction for diverse adolescent learners such as English language learners, writers with special needs, and high-performing writers.

4

✛

Brain Variation and Writing

INTRODUCTION AND CHAPTER OVERVIEW

Brain science and writer-teachers establish brain variation as the rule, not the exception, in writing classrooms. Adolescent writers walk, talk, read, and write with different brains, experiences, abilities, and ways of seeing the world. After illustrating brain variation from the perspective of brain science and writer-teachers, this chapter focuses on writing strategies to target three varying populations of adolescent writers: English language writers, special needs writers, and high-performing writers.

Even if your classroom does not have any of these student populations (I doubt if such a classroom exists!) the overriding message is that good writing instruction for targeted populations of students is good writing instruction for all students. These three areas of pedagogical expertise have a wealth of strategies and approaches to offer any teacher of writing.

THE SCIENTIFIC VIEW OF BRAIN VARIATION

Jake Gladstone exemplifies the varied, plastic nature of our brains. Jake is a four-year-old boy born with nearly half of his brain missing, likely due to a stroke suffered while in the womb. The image below shows an MRI scan of Jake's brain, the white being where cysts developed rather than brain matter.

Despite fears that Jake would never learn to walk or talk, his mother, Sarah, relates an experience that has been indicative of Jake's growing

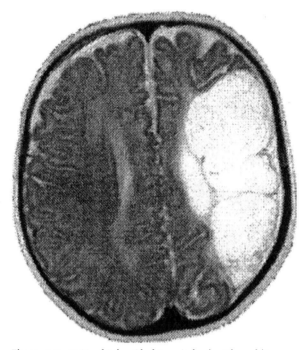

Figure 4.1. MRI of Jake Gladstone's brain. The white section on the right indicates where the cysts developed rather than brain matter as a result of a stroke suffered while he was in the womb.

abilities: "He pointed to my glass and said 'orange.' I couldn't believe it. He was walking and talking. It seemed like a miracle" (Laing, 2014).

Remarkably, there are several stories such as this where people born with or receiving extensive brain damage nevertheless go on to live healthy lives as the undamaged remaining brain compensates for missing or damaged portions of the brain. This plasticity of the brain, its ability to vary itself and adopt capabilities normally reserved for other areas, is inherent in each of our own unique brains.

There are insights to take away from the story of Jake Gladstone relevant to our discussion about brain variation and the implications for teaching writing to adolescent learners. First, the plastic nature of our brains means that all of us have unique brains, distinct from one another.

Evidence from brain science affirms the idea of brain variation, namely, that each of us has a unique brain. Nobel Prize recipient Eric Kandel explains that even identical twins "don't have identical brains and that is because learning leads to anatomical changes in the brain and even identical twins will have different social experiences, different learning experiences, and therefore will end up having different brains." Kandel summarizes: "Every single person in the world, as far as we know, has a slightly different brain than any other person because they've been exposed to somewhat different social and environmental experiences."

Another insight about the brain from the story of Jake Gladstone is that brain variation is a hallmark of human development. Brain variation is perhaps what most distinguishes humans from other animals. A reason why we have such brain variation is because of our extended developmental period, often referred to as neoteny (Choi, 2009). While other animals move quickly from childhood into adulthood (for example, mice are fully mature within a few weeks and chimpanzees are full grown by twelve to thirteen years), humans have a prolonged period of maturation lasting up to twenty-four years.

The advantage of this extended development, or neoteny, is that we have a longer period of time for our brains to adapt to our environments, especially given the fact that our brains are particularly responsive to learning before maturity. Our brains continue to learn and develop for a much longer amount of time and to a much greater degree than other animals.

The downside to having such plastic brains at birth is that it will be a long time before we can live autonomously, whereas other animals can forage for food and defend themselves against threat at a much earlier age. We have essentially traded the ability to mature quickly for the ability to be more adaptive and responsive to our environment.

A mark of human development expressly relevant to our discussion here is the stage of human adolescence. Adolescence is, in fact, exclusive to humans. While other animals move from childhood directly to adulthood, humans experience an additional growth spurt during adolescence (Bogin, 1999). The upside to this additional stage of development is that adolescence is a rich time for learning. We are biologically engineered for learning during adolescence. Rather than viewing adolescence as a period to rush through on our way to adulthood, adolescence should instead be seen for what it is: a distinctive evolutionary period in our natural human development.

The scientific view of brain variation teaches us that variation is what differentiates us from other animals. Brain variation is an adaptive, evolutionary advantage and the developmental period of adolescence is an especially unique time for humans. People like Jake Gladstone feature the brain's astonishing ability to vary itself even in response to extensive damage to the brain.

WRITER-TEACHERS SPEAK TO BRAIN VARIATION

Writer-teachers are keenly aware that different ways of thinking and seeing—i.e., brain variation—is what makes for strong writing. Diane Wakoski, a poet with more than twenty collections of poetry and thirty years of teaching experience, invokes Emily Dickinson's notion of "slant" to help convey the importance of thinking and writing in a personally unique manner:

> I think that what I try to do is invent something about that object that I'm looking at that is one unique to my way of thinking about it. There's Emily Dickinson's great word, she does own this word—slant—and it seems like a word that is almost numinous. . . . It's that vision that takes you. You're looking at the same thing everyone else is looking at, and it's not just point of view, it's the slant of it, and you in fact then use the visual object, not like a Rorschach test, and not exactly like a springboard to get you into the water, but you use it as the beginning of a meander through a map or a landscape.

Mike Rose reifies this idea of thinking and writing in a manner that is idiosyncratic, referencing what he calls "my vision." Rose reflects on his personal vision made concrete through writing: "It would be me, not totally unique obviously, other people are born in similar circumstances, but the particular twists and turns and all that, they happened to me and for better or for worse they are going to affect how I see things, the line of sight I take on things." While writer-teachers do not invoke the scientific terms of brain variation, developmental periods, or evolutionary biology, it is clear these writer-teachers recognize the value of variability in thinking and writing.

Mariah Fredericks, a writer of young adult novels, emphasizes the personal nature of writing when she says, "I feel like the act of writing is more core self." She argues, "Finding our own voice and being good at our own voice also can produce a really great book."

The end-goal for writing is not uniformity. Writing is a celebration of the personal. Even highly scripted genres such as lab reports and résumés are not meant to be identical. In this manner written products are a reflection of the brains that have produced them—each one with its own distinctive architecture resulting from varying inheritance, experience, and perspective.

BRAIN VARIATION AND TEACHING WRITING:
AN ASSET-BASED APPROACH

We don't need scientific reports to tell us that adolescent writers vary from one another—if our students all handed in the exact same paper we would be worried about plagiarism at best, alien abduction at worst. The greater point is that writing is a medium in which brain variation is on display.

The concept of brain variation from the sciences graphs well onto the educational concept of differentiation. Differentiation references the importance of taking into consideration the different cognitive styles and abilities of adolescent learners.

An essential insight when learning about differentiation is that, as a general rule, good teaching is good teaching for all students. While there is certainly value in having a degree in bilingual education or a certificate in special education, studies show that choosing good teachers to work with English language learners (ELLs) or students with special needs is more important than having a specialized degree (Loeb, Soland, and Fox, 2014).

This insight empowers us to intervene more fully with student populations even as we question our own expertise. Just as we know that writing must be taught by mathematics and art teachers as well as English and social studies teachers, good differentiation strategies should be employed by all teachers with all students. Adolescents learn best when their teachers treat their learning as a shared enterprise.

What follows in this chapter is discussion about providing effective feedback as a primary mode of differentiating for brain variation in the classroom. This is followed by several differentiation strategies grouped around three groups of adolescent writers: English language learners, writers with special needs, and high-performing writers.

Providing Effective Feedback

Before looking at strategies of differentiation within specific groups of students it's useful to overview the importance of differentiating feedback—a pedagogical move that meets the needs of all the various brains in your classroom. Here are several strategies for differentiating feedback that can make for better feedback and for more efficient expenditure of teacher time (the biggest detractor from providing feedback is usually the amount of time it takes):

- *The Rule of Three.* Limiting feedback is essential. All too often teachers of writing spend more time providing feedback than is necessary—

sometimes even spending more time providing feedback than the adolescent spent composing the text. As a general rule, you don't want to provide an adolescent writer with more than three points to improve his/her writing. Oftentimes, even one or two points are more than enough. Any more than three salient points of feedback cannot be taken thoughtfully into consideration.

- *Feedback Sweet Spot.* What one to three comments of feedback do you provide? These one to three points provided to the adolescent writer should be in the "feedback sweet spot"—just beyond what they can do but not too far into the territory of what they can't do yet to be most effective.

Figure 4.2.

- *Effectively Limit Grammar Corrections.* It is not the job of the writing teacher to copyedit. In fact, this does a disservice to adolescent writers when they revise since they are simply following directions as opposed to thinking through their own changes. A way to effectively limit grammar instruction is to check for grammar on a certain portion of a text. If the text is a page long, for example, comment on the grammar of one paragraph. If the text is several pages, consider commenting on the grammar of one page.

This strategy does a few things well. First, it limits the amount of time you have to expend correcting grammar. Second, it frees you up to think about the ideas in the writing without focusing solely on grammar. Third, when the adolescent revises the writing, he is provided with a model section that sets the bar for what the rest of the text should look like. Fourth, the adolescent will appreciate comments that deal with the ideas presented in the text rather than comments dominated by grammatical concerns.

- *The Importance of Timing.* When to provide feedback is an important decision that all too often teachers of writing get entirely wrong. Feedback provided on a finished assignment is a ubiquitous mistake. In the traditional model an adolescent writer turns in their finished draft and then receives feedback. What happens next? Usually the adolescent writer looks to the grade and then, if they are inclined to do so (which not every adolescent writer is), they look to the feedback from the teacher, which most often is provided to justify the grade.

Consider another more effective model of providing feedback: The adolescent writer turns in their draft and then receives feedback along with a "standing" or "moveable" grade based on the revisions the writer chooses to act upon. The feedback is written to help the adolescent writer improve the writing rather than justify the grade. The adolescent writer is then motivated to read the feedback in order to make changes to improve the writing and the eventual grade. The final draft is then given a higher grade (significant revisions), the same grade (little revisions), or a grade lower than the initial grade (insignificant or no revisions).

- *Conferencing as Feedback.* Conferencing with adolescent writers (i.e., meeting individually or with a small group of writers) is a highly effective means of providing feedback. It is advantageous to have a plan for the structure of the conference. Here are two example structures, the first in response to a first draft or "seed-idea" entry and the second responding to a second draft of a written work:

Conference with a first draft or seed-idea entry:

1. Have the writer read the entire entry or draft aloud.
2. Ask questions to help the writer to develop and discover the topic more fully, or help the writer to focus, or to find significance, or use qualities of good writing. Suggest model texts if appropriate.
3. End with an action plan appropriate for the writer's stamina, and a deadline for the second draft.

Conference with a second draft:

1. Have the writer read the entire draft of the assignment aloud.
2. Discuss the changes the student made from the first draft to the second draft. Keep in mind that the writer should do most of the explaining and talking. Have the writer explain the differences between the first and second draft and why these changes were made.
3. Ask the writer what it means to revise. What is good revision as opposed to bad revision? What is the writer's strategy for revising?
4. Ask what further changes should be made to the draft or whether the draft is complete. If further changes are warranted, discuss what these changes are and how they should be made. Come up with an action plan for further revision.

If the student feels the draft is complete, have the student explain why the paper is complete and why it is a reflection of their best work. Note: This is a carefully negotiated space. If the second draft clearly needs more work, then by all means encourage another revision. If the draft has met the assignment expectations, then encourage the writer to articulate why the assignment is complete and does not require further revision.

Two overarching guides to conducting effective conferencing have been mentioned and are worth revisiting. First, it is crucial to remember that the adolescent writer should be doing most of the talking during conferences. The pedagogical maxim being adhered to is that the person who is doing most of the talking is also doing most of the learning. Second, the outcome of the conference should be a well-articulated and recorded action plan agreed upon by you and the adolescent writer. Conferences are much less effective when the next steps are indefinite.

We now move on to discuss differentiation strategies appropriate for three different groups of writers: English language writers, special needs writers, and high-performing writers. Keeping in mind the insight that good teaching strategies work with all students, these strategies, while designed to be appropriate for these groups of writers, are suitable for all writers.

WRITING WITH ENGLISH LANGUAGE LEARNERS

The most important takeaway from this section is that learning a second language is an asset, not a deficit. All too often English language learners are marginalized in classrooms deemphasizing their first language and drawing undo attention to what they haven't yet mastered, haven't yet automatized in their writing. If we flip this thinking on its head we end up with a much more vibrant and useful approach to learning a second language.

Jhumpa Lahiri, winner of a Pulitzer Prize, presents the type of approach being advocated here toward learning a second language. Lahiri writes primarily in English but has recently been experimenting with writing in Italian. She describes this process of writing in a new language as "discovering this whole other room." She continues, "It's made me think a lot about language in general. I think that if a writer writes in more than one language, you really recognize how specific and complex a language is" (2013).

An asset-based approach toward teaching English language learners focuses on the fact that learning a second language informs the first language and vice versa. It is a pedagogical stance of celebrating the various languages in the writing classroom at all levels of proficiency—from those adolescent writers fluent in another language to those who may only know a few words.

In my own writing classroom this year I am fortunate to have ten different languages that my students speak fluently or have some rudimentary knowledge of. To celebrate this variety of language we count off for group work using a different language each time and we discuss the different traditions associated with languages such as wedding customs, holidays, and food preferences. Rather than treating English as an invisible, default mode of communication, a classroom celebrating language diversity is a classroom taking advantage of the variety of knowledge adolescent writers bring with them into the classroom.

What does learning a new language look like in the brain? We are far from knowing all the intimate details of second language acquisition but we do know that second languages look different in the brain depending on proficiency. While listening to stories in one's first language compared to one's second language, for example, low-proficiency learners showed much different cortical patterns between the first and second language. Highly proficient learners, in contrast, regardless of the age at which they learned their second language, showed no such major differences in brain activity between hearing their first and second languages (Perani et al., 1998).

This study of what first and second language acquisition looks like in the brain informs us that as the second language becomes more and more automatic the brain treats the two languages similarly. The goal of second language acquisition then should be to bring the native language into close proximity to the targeted second language. Unfortunately, this has not been the case as most classrooms emphasize the elimination of the first language in preference to the target language. A more useful model for teaching English language learners is one that uses the adolescent's first language as a bridge to English as opposed to treating the first language as an obstacle.

Fortunately, writing is a perfectly situated tool for building bridges between one's first and second language. Learning a first language starts with listening then leads into speaking, reading, and eventually writing. Second language acquisition, however, looks much different. Writing is often where the process of second language acquisition can start since English language learners "can spend more time thinking—searching for words and mentally translating—whereas when speaking, they are unable to do all these spontaneously. Thus, English language learners are able to say more in writing English than they can express in English orally" (Fu, 2009, 108–9).

Writing can also be used as a diagnostic indicator when working with English language learners. Since writing shows us a culmination of thinking as opposed to spontaneous or unscripted thinking represented by speech, writing shows what skills English language learners still need to develop not only for their writing but for their speaking and reading.

The following are strategies for working with English language learners:

- *Mixed Language Writing.* Mixed language writing takes advantage of using the native language as a bridge for successfully code switching into English. Mixed language writing runs along a spectrum from integrating a few English words into a majority of first language writing to integrating a few first language words into a majority of English writing. Mixed language writing can also take the form of double-entry writing, with the native language written on one side of the page and the English translation on the other side of the page.

A mixed language writing activity that I've used successfully with more proficient English language learners is called "Ten Words." In this writing assignment I ask writers to embed ten words from another language into their writing. The trick is to be sure that the meaning of each word can be ascertained through context clues provided. This is a fun activity for adolescent writers who can share their writing with a partner to see if the partner can guess the meaning of the words given the context clues provided.

- *Prewriting with Native Language.* Prewriting activities such as journaling, clustering, outlining, or freewriting are especially important for English language learners. Prewriting can take advantage of one's native language skills by intermixing native language with the target language of English. It should become evident over time that adolescent writers will begin to infuse more English into their prewriting as they continue to add English words to their lexicon.
- *Sentence Starters and Primes.* English language learners have a tendency to keep using one method that works over and over again. With less vocabulary to draw from, English language learners tend to resist new forms. The problem is that sentence variety, not grammatical correctness, is the sign of a mature writer. Sentence starters and primes urge English language learners into new forms of expression. Sentence starters, primes, and even vocabulary can be printed and placed in view on a classroom wall or student desks. Sentence starters can be created for specific writing occasions such as summary, argument, description, etc. Here are a some examples:
  - *Whole-Class Modeling.* English language learners develop their writing skills with the aid of modeling. Completing a writing assignment as a whole class models the writing together before adolescent writers strike

Sentence Starters for Writing a Conclusion

In summary…	In conclusion…
All things considered…	As has been demonstrated…
All in all…	As can be seen…
As should be clear by now…	Finally, it should be noted…
Ultimately…	It can be concluded that…

Sentence Primes for Integrating Counterclaims

While some may argue _____ , this is wrongheaded because…	The other side of the issue is _____ ; however…
While it is true that _____ , nevertheless…	Some refute the claims offered here based on _____ , but they are missing the point that…
There is another side to this story, namely, that _____ , however…	Although this argument appears sound, some point out_____ . This is misleading however because…

Figure 4.3.

out on their own. Whole-class modeling can come in a variety of shapes and sizes and can be done at different stages in the writing process.

For example, you may begin with a whole-class brainstorming session opening with a talk-aloud, jotting down notes on the board as they come to you before eliciting help from students. Or you may project a rough draft on the board and demonstrate your thinking as you revise. Or you may have a student project her draft and have the whole class join in the revision process.

Other iterations of whole-class modeling include beginning the writing together so that everyone has the same first paragraph that provides not only the topic of the writing but also the organizational structure that the rest of the writing will follow. Adolescent writers can then complete the writing on their own, checking later to see how their writing was different and similar to peers.

- *Language Goals Written into Lesson Plan.* A surefire way to integrate language instruction is to be explicit about language goals when writing lesson plans. What vocabulary will your students need to understand in order to grasp the lesson? How will students practice this vocabulary independently by speaking, reading, and writing? Language goals written into the lesson plan relate to much of what was discussed about the importance of explicitly teaching academic language in chapter 3.

- *Collaborate.* Collaborating with bilingual, ELL, and other teachers or aides is a necessary support for English language learners. It is not enough to have English language learners be pulled from class to work on their English skills. As argued earlier, parsing instruction is not a viable strategy. If you have an English language learner in your classroom you are by definition an English language teacher. If there is a specialist in your school who works with English learners this is a wonderful resource to collaborate on and learn from.

WRITING WITH SPECIAL NEEDS LEARNERS

I recently sat down for a talk with David Connors, a teacher of close to thirty years with experience teaching all content areas to students with learning disabilities in resource room, self-contained, and inclusive settings. He emphasized the significance of not falling back on a deficit lens when working with special needs learners.

The ideal special educator meets writers where they are, utilizing the writer's strengths to help them move forward. The essential approach is to become the bridge between the writer and the content objectives. This, of course, holds true for all settings; it just so happens this pedagogical approach is specifically featured when working with special needs learners.

While the degree of specialization required will change given the population of special needs learners, there are several strategies that can be helpful when working with special needs writers. Below are a few of these strategies:

- *Practice in Front and With.* The strategy of practicing and modeling writing for adolescent learners in front of and with them is particularly useful when working with special needs learners. Practicing and modeling in front and with helps surface the many steps in the writing process in real-time, chronological order. This type of "fishbowl" practicing and modeling allows the writing teacher to stop and check for understanding and gives time for students to pose questions.
- *Context for Writing.* Again, a strategy helpful for all adolescent writers, but especially adolescent writers with special needs, is to pro-

Acronym / Acrostic	Explanation
RAFT: Role of the Writer: Who are you as the writer? A movie star? The President? A plant? Audience: To whom are you writing? A senator? Yourself? A company? Format: In what format are you writing? A diary entry? A newspaper? A love letter? Topic: What are you writing about?	RAFT is a "big picture" acrostic designed to keep the writer afloat with all the different higher-order demands of writing. RAFT helps adolescent writers think through the writing process by posing the big questions that need to be answered in order to write effectively.
PIE: Point, Illustrations, Evidence	A manner of organizing an effective paragraph. Make a point, provide illustrations of that point, end with supporting evidence.
PER: Point, Evidence, Review	Another way of organizing an effective paragraph by making a point, providing evidence, and reviewing the point and evidence.
CROWN: Communicate what you learned; React personally to the lesson; Offer one sentence that sums up the lesson; Where can you use what you learned today? Note how well you did today	A closure technique that enables adolescents to reflect on a completed lesson in writing.
IDEAL: Identify, Define, Explore, Action, Look back	IDEAL is an acrostic which provides a process for solving problems: Identify the problem, Define the problem, Explore possible solutions and effects, Action the chosen solution, Look back at the results of the chosen solution.
STOPS: Sentence structure, Tenses, Organization, Punctuation, Spelling	Helpful for remembering grammatical areas to check when revising or reviewing.

Figure 4.4.

vide ample context for the writing event. Answering the questions of who/what/when/where/how contextualizes the meaningfulness of the writing assignment. Explicit teacher-to-student and peer-to-peer conversations about what will happen in the writing are valuable uses of classroom instructional time, providing a fuller context for writing.

As I'm sure you have discovered or intuited in your own teaching, asking adolescents to write on demand is rarely successful. Warming the waters by providing a rich context for writing is a much better strategy to get the best writing out of your adolescent writers, especially those with special needs.

- *Acronyms and Acrostics.* Always remember to BID (Break It Down). It is especially important to break down complex learning activities like writing into manageable component parts for special needs learners. The special education teacher, from whom we can all learn, is particularly skillful at this process.

Acronyms and acrostics help facilitate self-directed writing goals. The built-in mnemonic nature of acronyms and acrostics helps adolescents remember various steps when writing. Figure 4.4 provides a few examples.

- *Collaborative Goal Setting.* Setting goals in collaboration with special needs learners for their writing differentiates instruction and provides accountability. Goals can also be set in collaboration with peers. Being realistic about goals is essential as goals can range from integrating more sources into one's writing to completing one full paragraph of writing. While goals can be reached via dialogue, collaboratively set goals should be recorded in writing for the sake of clarity and accountability.

A few concluding remarks about working with special needs writers are in order. Special needs writers often have a heightened sense of wanting to be appropriately challenged. This means special needs writers have low tolerance for work that is clearly "dumbed down," alongside a low tolerance for work that is too challenging or overwhelming. Finding appropriately challenging writing tasks is a consistently negotiated practice. Sometimes you will find the ideal task and sometimes you will not. It is therefore necessary to continually seek feedback from your special needs writers.

It is important to remember that all writers can continue to develop and improve. Mike Rose says of special needs writers:

I think you can school people to quite a high level of performance in just about anything given basic certain requirements. If someone is born with brain damage then clearly there's going to be a ceiling but that ceiling may be much higher than people think. We have those extraordinary stories of mothers who say, "No I absolutely refuse to put my kid in a home" and so the kid becomes higher functioning. So the upper limits of human potential and performance can always be pushed.

WRITING WITH HIGH-PERFORMING WRITERS

This statement from a practicing teacher is all too common: "In my school I feel as if there is a lot of support and options for high-needs students, but not enough for students who are meeting or exceeding standards." This teacher goes on to argue quite correctly that, "No matter the level, students can always improve."

How do we improve the writing of high-performing adolescent writers? Here are some strategies to enact and some strategies to avoid when targeting this oft neglected population of writers:

- *Inductive Teaching.* Inductive as opposed to deductive teaching is especially appropriate for high-performing writers. An inductive approach provides adolescent writers with a strong model and asks them to analyze the parts that make up the whole. For example, adolescent writers may be provided an argumentative piece of writing that they can then analyze for the different techniques and strategies deployed to make such an argument.
- In contrast to the inductive teaching approach, a *deductive approach* is more teacher-centered wherein the teacher picks out the techniques and strategies, which are then made explicit to the adolescent writers. Inductive teaching, on the whole, is more writer centered as it asks the adolescent writers to analyze the effectiveness of a given model or even search for their own models.
- *Encourage Risk Taking.* High-performing writers are usually proud of their abilities and can become reluctant risk takers because what they are already doing has proven successful. Therefore, it is important to alleviate any fears of getting something "wrong" and to encourage high-performing writers to take risks. Again, the mark of a mature writer is the cultivation of a wide repertoire of writing strategies, not the cultivation of a perfectly polished narrow skill set.

One way to encourage risk taking is to challenge high-performing writers with feedback, not grades. There is no rule saying feedback and grades must be directly correlated. An "A" paper can still receive critical feedback just as a "C" or "D" paper can have feedback encouraging the writer. High-performing writers are often intrinsically motivated writers so critical feedback is a particularly effective strategy.

- *Flexible Approach toward Writing Assignments.* High-performing writers will often want to personalize their approach toward a writing assignment or go above and beyond set guidelines. In most cases this can be encouraged as long as the writer can communicate her intentions clearly. Having a flexible approach toward writing assignments should not equate to open-ended, rudderless assignments with no clear objectives, goals, or assessments. Flexibility can go hand in hand with clear criteria that should be agreed upon collaboratively.

- *Group Writing Projects.* High-performing writers tend toward working autonomously and independently. While this is not always negative, high-performing writers must learn to work successfully with other adolescent writers. Well-designed group writing projects in which every member of the group is responsible for contributing to the writing is a pedagogically rich context for learning how to work alongside peers.

- *What NOT to Do.* There are a few strategies when working with high-performing writers that get overemphasized. High-performing writers should not always be working independently. Working independently is probably what most of your high-performing writers are used to and unfortunately have come to prefer. This, however, does a disservice to their social development as they miss out on social interactions in the classroom.

High-performing writers should also not always be the teacher's aide or be assigned to improve the writing of other students. While there are virtues to these roles, high-performing writers in your classroom are still adolescents who need to learn to work alongside peers effectively and need encouragement to continue developing their own writing as opposed to believing they have reached the finish line.

When I teach freshman composition courses—the first writing course adolescent learners take out of high school—I invariably have students who feel deceived by their high school experiences where their writing was always given praise and the highest marks. These students must overcome their own inflated sense of writing competence in order to roll up their sleeves and get to work further developing their writing.

In contrast, many students in these first-year writing courses come in as excellent writers along with a helpful attitude that writing is hard work and requires continuous development. This attitude services high-performing writers in their college experience much more than an attitude that they have always been a "gifted" or "natural" writer.

A few big ideas run throughout our discussion of the various adolescent populations highlighted in this chapter. First and foremost, good instruction—whether for English language learners, writers with special needs, high-performing writers, or mainstream students—is good instruction for all students.

Second, it is important to remember that not all English language learners are the same just as not all special needs or gifted students are the same. Brain variation rules the landscape in any classroom, especially those classrooms making an earnest effort at teaching writing.

Finally, writing is an ideal activity for all adolescent learners precisely because of its ability to differentiate, to meet the learners where they are. Thankfully, writing has an extremely low entry point and no ceiling. Writing is a skill that's easy to begin but impossible to master, which makes writing an ideal activity for classrooms emphasizing brain variation.

BRAIN VARIATION AND WRITING: CONNECTIONS TO THE ENGLISH LANGUAGE ARTS WRITING COMMON CORE STATE STANDARDS

The strategies offered in this chapter are designed to help all adolescents reach the writing goals set by the CCSS. The goal of *Providing Effective Feedback*, for example, is highly malleable and capable of meeting each of the CCSS as the feedback provided can be catered to meet any standard. Providing Effective Feedback is particularly appropriate for standards mentioning revision such as: "Develop and strengthen writing as needed by planning, revising, editing, rewriting, or trying a new approach, focusing on addressing what is most significant for a specific purpose and audience" (CCSS.ELA-Literacy.11-12.5).

Several strategies in this chapter are equally as malleable and can therefore be responsive to any given standard. These strategies include: *Whole-Class Modeling, Language Goals Written into Lesson Plan, Practice in Front and With, Acronyms and Acrostics,* and *Collaborative Goal Setting*. Each of these strategies can be constructed to focus on one or more of the CCSS.

Lastly, *Sentence Starters and Primes* is an effective means of teaching specific aspects of writing such as the syntax of transitional sentences and conclusions as called for by these CCSS:

- "Use words, phrases, and clauses as well as varied syntax to link the major sections of the text, create cohesion, and clarify the relationships between claim(s) and reasons, between reasons and evidence, and between claim(s) and counterclaims." (CCSS.ELA-Literacy.11-12.1.C)
- "Provide a concluding statement or section that follows from or supports the argument presented." (CCSS.ELA-Literacy.11-12.1.E)

WHERE WE'VE BEEN AND WHERE WE'RE GOING

This chapter illustrates and explores the concept of brain variation, establishing brain variation as the rule rather than exception in our classrooms. Brain science and testimonials from writer-teachers converge to support a view of brain variation, a view that each of us possesses unique brain architecture based on distinct social experiences coupled with unique biological design.

A writing classroom aware of brain variation is a writing classroom that strives to differentiate instruction for adolescent learners. This chapter supplies a number of strategies to support differentiated writing instruction across various student populations.

The next chapter, *Positive Affect and Writing*, discusses the symbiotic relationship between emotions and learning. This is a well-documented, productive area of overlap between brain science and education. The strategies provided seek to place student engagement at the center of writing instruction.

5

✛

Positive Affect and Writing

INTRODUCTION AND CHAPTER OVERVIEW

If this chapter had an exclamatory motto it would be: "Writing should be fun!" Beginning teachers are often criticized for writing lessons that over-emphasize fun, whereas veteran teachers often go too far in the reverse direction by not making time in their lessons for motivation and fun.

This chapter begins by making the case that fun—i.e., positive affect—goes hand in hand with learning. Positive affect is in fact a necessary first step in teaching writing and results in better cognition, better writing. Several strategies are offered to promote positive affect in writing instruction.

BRAIN SCIENCE AND THE VALUE OF POSITIVE AFFECT

Consider how your mind operates when stressed or anxious. How much conscious control can you exert over your thoughts? Compare moments of stress to other times when you are relaxed or positively engaged—how does your mind operate differently within these states?

As with most of us, stress and anxiety provoke responses that overtake our ability to think and to reason effectively, making learning difficult and creative pursuits nearly impossible. In the face of stress or anxiety the amygdala signals the brain's control center, the hypothalamus, which in turn releases adrenaline and our heart rate quickens, senses are height-ened, breathing increases. These conditions are good things when, say, facing an oncoming car. These conditions are not so good, however, when sitting down to write.

Brain science has long recognized the connection between mood (i.e., affect) and cognitive performance. Negative affective states such as anxiety and stress lead to poor cognitive performance. The opposite is also quite true and presents us with a key insight to harness when teaching writing: Positive affect correlates with improved cognitive performance.

A number of studies have been performed illustrating the relationship between positive affect and cognition. As an example, a study with adolescent learners was conducted around a word-generation task. In this task the adolescents were asked to write down as many words as they could related to the topic of "fruits and birds" within a set period of time.

Half the adolescents in this study were complimented on their appearance (clothing, hair, etc.) and given a small gift (a pack of gum) before completing the word-generation task. The other half of adolescents were complimented and given a small gift after completing the word-generation task. Those adolescents primed with positive affect before the task outperformed those primed after the task (Greene and Noice, 1988).

Many such experiments have similarly displayed the effects of positive affect on cognitive and creative tasks. More recent work in brain science has been able to benefit from fMRI technology to locate areas in the brain coordinated with positive affect. Mark Beeman (2014) at Northwestern University, for example, has conducted studies looking at the brain while performing a cognitive task in a state of positive affect. He and his collaborators have drawn attention to an area of the brain called the anterior cingulate cortex (ACC).

The ACC shows an interesting pattern of activity. The ACC is initially active in response to positive affect. The ACC is then primed by positive affect to facilitate creative problem solving, especially problems that require insight or "thinking outside the box" for a solution.

This brings up another important piece of knowledge from brain science, namely, that creativity is not a singular cognitive process. At the very least, creativity requires a vacillation between two very different modes of creative thought: focused cognition and defocused cognition.

Focused cognition is what we usually think of as "hard thinking" or deliberate, analytic thinking, whereas defocused cognition is sudden insight, "thinking outside the box," "Aha!," "Eureka!," associative thinking. The high mark of a creative thinker, and by extension the successful writer, is knowing when and how to navigate back and forth between these convergent and divergent patterns of thought.

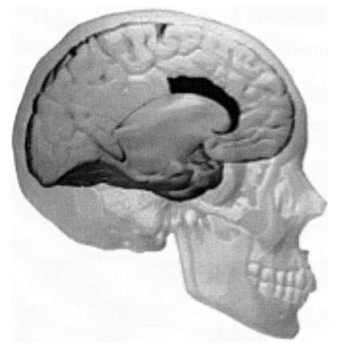

Figure 5.1. Anterior Cingulate Cortex

WRITER-TEACHERS SPEAK TO POSITIVE AFFECT

Writer-teachers speak to a number of positive emotions within their writing process. Three emotions were especially predominant when looking across the interviews: having fun with writing, the pleasure of producing and creating something new, and the intrinsic drive to communicate with an audience.

In speaking with writer-teachers there is no shortage of comments referencing the positive experiences of writing. One question—"What does writing give back to you?"—was quite effective in eliciting the positives of writing. Deborah Brandt shares: "The act of writing is magic. I want to write. If I could be writing every hour of the day I would." She caps this off by saying, "Writing is just so much fun."

Writing as fun is a theme revisited time and again in these interviews with writer-teachers. James Gee says, "I write because it's fun. This last year I played video games a lot and I play them because they're fun. I write because it's fun and I realize that right now writing is the only activity I find more fun than video games." When writing is enjoyable and fun these writer-teachers are receiving the advantages of a mind working within positive affect, which we now understand to improve cognitive performance.

Mariah Fredericks shares another advantage of enjoying the writing process, the fact that if the writer is enjoying herself that enjoyment will transfer into the writing: "If you're enjoying yourself, somebody else is going to enjoy it, too. You know, Stephenie Meyer [author of the Twilight series] didn't wake up and say, 'I know. Mormon vampires.' She loves that story, you can tell. I think that connection of the writer loving the story helps the reader love the story." Fredericks believes the writer must enjoy the writing in order to breathe a healthy vitality into the writing, which is ultimately experienced by readers.

Fredericks highlights the importance of being excited and joyful about writing when she speaks to her approach to teaching as well: "What I tried to share with [students] is how to get excited about writing and have a lot of fun with it, to make it be the best part of your day, where you get to sit and scribble out your story, and if that story is your suburban mother is an axe murderer, then fabulous." For Fredericks the subject of the writing is not as impactful as the approach the writer takes toward the writing, again highlighting the value of positive affect in the writing process.

The biggest draw for taking up writing as a career for writer-teachers is the positive benefits associated with producing and creating. These writer-teachers feel the deep pleasure of creation. Deborah Brandt describes: "It's crafting, it's making something and that gives me a lot of pleasure." Art Markman simply states, "I like to produce stuff," concluding, "For me in fact any kind of writing is one of the more rewarding things I can do."

James Gee picks up this theme of writing as producing and creating by calling writing "a design challenge." Gee laments that schooling does not offer enough opportunities for students to be designers and creators, emphasizing instead a culture of consumption over production. "A lot of our education does not lead you to think of yourself as a producer but just as a consumer," he says, continuing, "Even when you're writing you're supposed to be writing to what people want you to do." Gee emphasizes thinking "like a designer" when writing to escape the dominant gestalt of consumption and helping students become producers, originators, creators.

Another positive drive writer-teachers discuss is the inherent worth of communicating with an audience. Deborah Brandt shares that writing is taken up by readers in ways that can't be anticipated, "and so it keeps living and I like that." Adam Higginbotham agrees with Brandt, saying: "There's a great deal of satisfaction in being able to bring some of this stuff to a wider audience and you get kind of recognition for doing that and recognition for doing it properly." Higginbotham goes on to share an anecdote illustrating the positive effects of communicating with a wider audience:

> One of the best things that's ever happened to me is I was riding the subway in the middle of last week and coming in from Brooklyn and a guy got on the subway, sat right down next to me reading [*The New Yorker*] and I looked over and he was reading the story that I had written. I sat there for a couple of stops thinking he's possibly audibly going to say, "Fuck it," and turn the page in frustration rather than go on reading something that's boring. But he didn't do that and then I just thought, "Well, I really can't let this go." So I tapped him on the shoulder and said, "Excuse me. Are you enjoying that?" and in a rather guarded way he said, "Yes." I was like, "Well, I wrote that." He was incredibly pleased with this and it was great.

Writer-teachers make visible a concept made popular by psychologist Steven Pinker (1994), namely, the language instinct—the idea that language is an instinct developed in humans to aid communication. Communication is thus seen as an innate drive and fulfilling this drive is pleasurable.

These writer-teachers illustrate the fun of writing, the gratification associated with producing and creating, and the inherent drive we share to communicate with an audience. These aspects of writing result in positive mood and affect, which, as we see from the evidence of brain science, improves cognitive performance. These writer-teachers tap into a win-win relationship wherein the writing creates positive affect, which in turn creates better writing. The next step in this discussion is to preview strategies, which help adolescent writers develop this positive relationship within their writing process.

THE VALUE OF FUN:
POSITIVE AFFECT AND TEACHING WRITING

There are a number of writing strategies to be used with adolescent writers to help take advantage of the cognitive gains from positive affect. The writing strategies shared in this section are designed to promote successful vacillation between focused and defocused thinking, engagement and fun, the challenge of creating and producing something new, and communication with an authentic audience. As these themes are interrelated, the strategies presented most often pick up several of these themes at once to promote positive affect in the adolescent writing classroom.

- *Focused and Defocused Thinking*. These two different ways of problem solving, of creating something new, are important benchmarks for adolescent cognition. As opposed to being a structured classroom writing strategy per se, focused and defocused thinking are modes of thought to be applied to a variety of writing contexts.

As an example, working with the constraints of a given genre can be seen as focused, analytic thinking. It is necessary to understand the requirements of a given genre and adhere to its rules and expectations. Defocused thinking comes into play when a genre may not be the appropriate fit for what is trying to be communicated. Adolescents need encouragement to both work within the constraints of a given genre (focused thinking) and to question whether or not the given constraints of a genre are appropriate for what it is they are trying to convey (defocused thinking).

As another example, it is important to periodically check in with adolescent writers in the midst of a writing project to find out if they would like to start over again. This question rarely gets asked. In my own experience, adolescent writers who have already begun a writing project and are sometimes fairly deep into the process suddenly realize "it's not working" for any number of reasons and wish they could start over with a new topic.

Starting over should be encouraged as it demonstrates writing as a learning process and shows that sometimes you need to be willing to discard what you've written and begin again with the knowledge gained from a first attempt. Adjusting deadlines collaboratively is a small price to pay for the gains adolescent writers receive from starting a writing project anew.

- *Choice.* Strong writers are intrinsically motivated. If you want the best writing from your adolescent writers you must provide them with choice and encourage them to take personal ownership over their writing. Studies continue to show that intrinsic motivation beats out extrinsic motivation every time. Offering adolescents choices about topics, genre, and even deadlines fosters a personal connection to writing.
- *Games and Cooperative Competition.* Competition in the classroom is a controversial topic and if you've ever tried incorporating competition into your teaching you probably know why. Adolescents can get competitive quickly, to both positive and negative effects. A positive includes the fact that competition heartily engages most students; a negative includes the fact that competition often involves winning and losing and adolescent students do not like to lose. Nevertheless, there are a number of classic games and cooperative competitions that can take advantage of the competitive spirit without resulting in hurt feelings.

- *Debate with Note Passing*. Debate in classrooms has a long history with endless variety. To focus on writing within classroom debates, have adolescents divide into small groups and choose a "talking head" to represent the group's ideas. During the debate group members can pass written notes to their talking head to make points. This turns the debate into a writing-on-your-feet activity. A variation is to have each group's talking head only be allowed to read the notes verbatim. Observers of the debate can act as judges, writing up what they believe are the strong and weak points made by each side.
- *Jeopardy*. A classic classroom game, Jeopardy is used by teachers across the content areas to review essential content information. Rather than having the teacher create the Jeopardy clues, however, this activity breaks adolescents into small groups to create the clues, understanding that different dollar amounts awarded should coincide with the difficulty of the content clues provided. This works especially well as a test-preparation activity.

Creating the Jeopardy clues is what makes this a writing-intensive activity as adolescents compose what they believe to be essential content knowledge around a given unit of study. Once the game has begun, the creators of the game are quick to find out which clues work and which don't—useful information for the next time they create a Jeopardy game.

- *Taboo*. Just as with the Jeopardy game, the popular game of Taboo can be engineered to focus on writing. In the traditional Taboo game, the objective is for a player to guess the correct word as teammates shout out clues without using the target word and five additional words listed on a card. In this reinvention of the game, the objective is for a player to guess the correct word with written clues from teammates (this also makes for a quieter game as teammates are not permitted to shout clues, only write them).

For example, a team might receive a card with "Watch" written at the top as the target word with the additional words to avoid posted beneath: Look, Time, Wrist, Clock, Wears. This team would then have a set period of time (a minute or two) to write up a list of words that will hopefully provoke their teammate to say the word "Watch" after reading.

This game helps adolescent writers expand their vocabulary by thinking past the words provided. The target words provided can be drawn from vocabulary lists, class readings, course concepts, etc.

- *Wordplay*. An easy strategy, wordplay asks adolescents either individually or in small groups to come up with as many words as they can using only the letters of a given word within a set period of time. For example, there are twenty-six word combinations within the word "writing." (Websites can provide a list of word combinations to be found within words.) The person or group with the most word combinations wins.

As with the Taboo game, a variation is to choose a given word drawn from vocabulary lists, class readings, course concepts, etc. Additional variations include only counting words that are three letters or longer and giving additional points to words that are uncommon (extra points awarded to any word that no one else repeated, for example). This strategy is particularly applicable in mathematics classrooms where words can be given frequency ratings and corresponding point values.

- *Scattergories.* Another word-generation game, Scattergories has adolescents come up with as many words as they can around a given topic such as "Elizabethan" or "photosynthesis." This works well in small groups where teams compete for how many original words they can write down. In this game repetition across groups is typically not allowed so that the goal becomes to record more unique word associations.

Variations include limiting the letter that words can begin with, which makes the game more manageable in terms of originated words. For example, "Come up with as many words associated with 'Elizabethan' starting with the letter 'E'." Another variation is to have each group come up with a sentence for their originated words, a sentence expressing each word's relationship to the topic provided.

- *Board Races.* This is a fun, adaptable, cooperative competition game that can get noisy. Here's how it works: Create a list of writing tasks that you want your adolescent writers to perform on the board. For example, you could ask them to write a sentence using a certain vocabulary word, fix the grammatical errors in a sentence provided, write a four-sentence paragraph on a given topic, find a quotation from the reading that supports or counters a given claim, use a certain sentence structure such as "I used to think _____, but now I think_____."

There are any number of possibilities. Print out your writing tasks (two copies if you plan to divide the class in half and more copies if you want several smaller groups) and then set up the Board Races game. Each team gets in a straight line facing the board. The board has a column for each team to work within. The first person in each line comes up to the board and is given a copy of the writing tasks. This person starts in the "reading" role. The second person is given chalk/marker to start in the "writing" role. The rest of the group members can help the writer verbally.

The game begins when the teacher signals the readers to read aloud the first instruction. Once the writer has written out the group's response, the writer switches into the reading role and the reader goes to the back of the line and the person at the front of the line becomes the next writer. Everyone cycles through until each has been in the writing role at least once. The first group to finish wins as long as, upon inspection, answers are correct, complete, and legible.

- *Essay Jumble.* This is a useful activity for teaching organizational structure. The Essay Jumble begins with an essay promoting the type of structure you want to communicate to your adolescent writers. Print out each paragraph onto a separate sheet of paper and hand them out to small groups of writers out of order. The object of this game is to assemble the essay in its correct order. A variation on this activity is to have one or two missing paragraphs that need to be written to complete the essay.
- *Class Collection.* Collaborative writing projects like a class collection is a way to solidify classroom culture and present finished work to an outside audience. Pride is inextricably linked to writing and a class collection of best work is a way to share with parents, extended relatives, and friends. As one adolescent writer discusses in a writing conference with his teacher: "I want to work on [my writing]. I want to feel better—proud." The more strategies we can enact that help adolescent writers feel a sense of pride in their writing, the more positive affect they will bring to their writing.
- *Class Newspaper.* Another strategy emphasizing collaboration and communication, creating a class newspaper is a way to get adolescents writing toward a common goal. A class newspaper can have one or several editions published and distributed and can be in hard copy, digital, or both. Class newspapers can reflect news of the entire school or news of the classroom. A simplified version is to create a class newsletter that can be sent home to parents each semester, month, or even week.
- *All Writing Is Story.* Storytelling organizational structures come naturally to adolescent writers, much more so than, say, research paper or lab report structures. For this reason it's promising to share the fact that behind every genre is a story to tell. In school-based writing this story takes the form of sharing your own learning and development around a topic. Table 5.1 shows two examples of research paper in-

Table 5.1.

Ask Me Later: Understanding and Dealing with Procrastination	*Bamboo Star: Origins and Practices of Chinese Childrearing*
To sit down and solve twenty math questions after a long day of school is a struggle for many students. After hours of taking notes we feel we cannot function and do another essay. As a result, before we start our homework we decide to watch television or, mostly these days, play around with social media applications. Examples of these include Facebook, Instagram, and YouTube. The availability of these products at the palm of our hands makes it very easy to succumb to procrastination and delay our work. This process of getting distracted and not doing work is relevant to many people's lives, especially students like myself. Unfortunately, this process is also a major problem because delaying work can lead to the work not getting done at all or work of low quality. We are still growing, so we are still learning the effects of making bad decisions such as procrastinating. The prevalence of this issue to our everyday lives pushed me to look further into what it is, why we do it, and how to stop it.	Since moving to America thirteen years ago, adults around me have called me a "bamboo star." I didn't understand what it meant nor did I question it. I simply accepted the name and assumed it was because bamboos are native to Asia and I am, of course, a star. But as I grew older, it became more apparent through experiences that losing my Chineseness might be beneficial. Occasionally, when I wanted to do something my parents disapproved of, such as staying up late to watch television, I would tell them, "I'm American, I'm free to do what I want." Their response has always been, "Is that what they teach you in school?" In retrospect, what I said was crude but not because I felt entitled and certainly not because I thought of myself as an American. My desire to understand this conflict prompted my decision to interview my parents and subsequently learn about childrearing practices of Chinese parents and the origins of their practices.

troductions that tell the story of why the topic was chosen and what is going to be learned through the process of writing.

These two writers are utilizing storytelling elements within the research paper genre by sharing why they are interested in the topic, their personal experiences with the topic, and what they hope to learn about their topic in their researching and writing. Understanding that all writing is a type of storytelling opens up an accessible entry point for adolescent writers into unfamiliar genres and genres that have long been considered overly abstract and impenetrable. Viewing all writing as storytelling casts writing in a more familiar and therefore positive light.

- *Snowball.* The snowball activity is a way to energize the classroom and can be used to review information learned, ask questions, or make predictions. Here's how it works: Responses or questions are written onto a small sheet of paper, which is then crumpled into a snowball and tossed into the center of the classroom. Each student then retrieves a snowball and responds in writing. There are many ways to vary this activity, including pausing at set intervals to share out as a whole class. This activity stresses writing to communicate with an audience and of course the fun of tossing "snowballs" around the room.

- *Favorite Words.* Encourage adolescent writers to take emotional possession of words to bolster positive affect when writing. There are several ways to do this such as creating lists of favorite words and sharing with classmates, choosing favorite words from a vocabulary list, identifying favorite words used in an article or book, etc. Adolescents can share their favorite word lists with one another to find similarities and differences, opening up discussion around word choice in written texts.

Creating lists of favorite words helps to promote a connection to language by underscoring a personal rather than "correct" answer and drawing attention to language at its most finely tuned, micro level. Discussions around favorite words transition well into discussion of words that are overused and become clichéd as well as words with unique designs such as palindromes, onomatopoetic words, and root words. Understanding root words such as "graph," "geo," "aqua," and "audio," for example, can help students unpack the meaning of associated words and provide insight into how language advances.

- *Shouldwords.* Adolescent writers enjoy creating their own words that should be words—shouldwords. Examples include "newfeel" (taking something out of the box for the first time) and "convolecture" (a lecture that includes lots of conversation). Adolescents enjoy creating these words and having the class guess at their intended meanings. Shouldwords are most often combinations of words or in some way onomatopoetic as they get across a certain type of emotion with their cadence. Just like favorite-words activities, creating shouldwords focuses adolescent attention on the finer nuances of language and, of course, it's fun.
- *Generational Words and Phrases.* Try observing adolescents without them knowing you are there or caring if you are there—adolescents in their unadulterated "natural" habitat. One thing you will notice is their use of language as they clearly talk differently than adults using different words and phrases. Every generation creates their own buzz words and phrases, at times sounding as though they speak another language. This is a rich subject for discussion. Have ado-

lescents share the words, phrases, and abbreviations they use with peers but not with adults.

What do these words and phrases mean? Why are they reserved for certain populations and not others? Answering these questions and writing about this shift in language use opens up discussions of code-switching, audience, accent, creole language, pidgin language, language flexibility, and even the creation of new language.

- *Magnet Poetry.* Most people are familiar with the popular magnet poetry activity where a given set of words are combined to create various intended meanings (usually on a refrigerator or other metal surface). A variation of this activity, especially useful if you don't have magnets, is simply to use index cards or words printed and then cut out. This also creates a more dynamic set of words that can be pulled from class materials.

A variation on magnet poetry is to have students align their words against the backdrop of a blank sheet of paper on which they can add words between the given magnet words, thus creating a more complex poem or paragraph of writing. Adolescent writers enjoy sharing and explaining their finished pieces, which successfully links positive engagement to class vocabulary.

- *Found Poetry.* Found poetry is similar to magnet poetry except the adolescents are responsible for creating their own word banks from which to draw. Adolescents can scour classroom resources such as bulletin boards, reading materials, notes, new vocabulary lists, etc. As with magnetic poetry, found poetry results in adolescent writers positively engaging with classroom materials. An extension of this activity asks adolescent writers to write a paragraph in which they include their found words.
- *Prewriting Fun.* Priming adolescent writers with fun prewriting activities is only limited by your imagination. For example, to teach descriptive writing try bringing in several paper bags filled with different textures such as cotton, sand, paper clips, flower petals— anything and everything that has a distinct texture. Without looking into the bags, adolescents can take turns placing their hands inside the bags and describing the textures orally and then in writing.

For compare/contrast writing assignments try bringing in two or three different types of plants for adolescents to view, touch, smell. For observation assignments treat the school as a laboratory and have adolescents eavesdrop on conversations. Try having adolescents study the advertisements they see on their way to school or within their favorite shows to highlight persuasive marketing writing and how it is designed to attract consumers. Try incorporating music, dance, painting, photography, or any combination thereof; having fun with creating prewriting activities ensures that your adolescent writers will have fun as well.

- *Describe a Scene.* Try this activity in which small groups choreograph and present a scene from a class reading. As each scene is presented, classmates in the audience describe the scene in writing. Variations include making the scene silent and having the audience write out their best guesses for dialogue, or the written descriptions must emphasize a particular aspect of writing such as objective description, active verbs, or adjectives. Descriptive reactions can also be written from various perspectives such as another character from the reading.

A popular variation has adolescents or the teacher creating a still scene for audience members to describe in writing. The still scene is created using adolescent volunteers from the class. This strategy works well when the scene is a representation of a scene from a class reading.

- *Show and Tell.* Ask your adolescent writers to bring in examples of their favorite writing. Oftentimes the writing we "count" in schools is limited to the printed word. This activity opens up writing to any platform, especially digital platforms where adolescents are likely to do most of their reading. Writing can also come in the form of song lyrics, comics, subtitled films, and video games.

Once adolescents bring in examples of their favorite writing they can analyze how the writing is operating. A set of questions/directions helps to unpack the writing: Summarize the writing. What is the form, or genre, of the writing? Who is speaking in the writing? What are the dominant images in the writing? What is the central idea in the writing? What makes the writing persuasive? How does the writing provoke an emotional response? What is the best technique used in the writing?

The final step in this activity is to encourage adolescent writers to incorporate the techniques of their favorite writing into their own writing. Analyzing the writing surfaces these techniques. A variation is to compose an apprentice text using the piece of favorite writing as a model.

- *Pen Pals.* We have all heard of this writing strategy and may even have our own memories of writing to a pen pal. This strategy does several things well including harnessing an authentic audience for clear peer-to-peer communication. The key element to pulling off a successful pen pal experience is organization. A popular and logistically sound pen pal experience begins with pairing up with another classroom. This could be a classroom down the hall, across the country, or across the world. Regardless of where your partner classroom is, this makes for an easy one-time mailing of all your letters without needing to keep track of several addresses.

There should be clear communication between teachers about the expectations of the writing. This is a time to collaborate on shared goals for the pen pal experience, which can be as loose as having writers share personal experiences to having writers talk explicitly about classroom content. Social studies and geography classes, for example, may want writers to share and ask questions about the different cultures across the classrooms, which can become an invigorated subject of study.

Be sure to brainstorm ideas as a whole class about what should be covered in a first letter, and active reading strategies should be explicitly taught. Writers should begin their letters by summarizing and responding to the letter received before writing about their own experiences/perspectives. Word count should be explicitly discussed and enforced as well since you don't want an adolescent writing ten pages and getting a one-line response. A culminating event such as a "last" letter, meeting in person, or meeting by conference call or Skype should take place as a capstone event (although writers should be encouraged to keep their communication going if they express interest).

- *Chainstories.* The most common way chainstories work is to have every writer begin a story with a line or full paragraph. This is then passed to another writer to add the next line or paragraph and so on until a set number of passes has been completed or the original writer gets her story back. The fun of chainstories is adding something new to each story received and reading where different writers have taken your own story beginning. Like most of the activities offered here, chainstories have a number of possible variations.

There aren't usually very many guidelines attached to chainstories but there certainly could be in order to connect this activity to course-content goals. For example, chainstories can be kept over a longer period of time, say, over the course of a unit of study. Each week writers can be responsible for adding something to a story that they have learned that week from the unit. Some chainstories could even be open for an entire semester or year. As with all of the activities targeting positive affect, this activity can be augmented to maintain the fun while also realizing content goals and standards.

Chainstories can be designed to include more content. Try having adolescent writers create chainstories wherein each line they add to the story has to contain a certain vocabulary word or class concept.

- *Just Ask.* Not the most revolutionary teaching strategy but one that works: Just ask adolescents what they enjoy writing. This conversation can provide valuable insights into what adolescents enjoy about the writing process as well as surface some misguided beliefs about writing that can be addressed. Another positive with this strategy is that asking adolescents what they like to write and then building a writing assignment from there is a means to achieve buy-in. Adolescents, just like all of us, will perform with more enthusiasm after knowing they have been heard and have shaped the direction of the writing to be completed.

POSITIVE AFFECT AND WRITING: CONNECTIONS TO THE ENGLISH LANGUAGE ARTS WRITING COMMON CORE STATE STANDARDS

Games and Cooperative Competitions can be catered to meet specific standards. *Debate with Note Passing*, for example, is a strategy emphasizing: "Write arguments focused on discipline-specific content" (CCSS. ELA-Literacy.WHST.11-12.1). This strategy meets the standards' articulation of introducing "knowledgeable claim(s)" and "supplying the most relevant data and evidence."

Board Races is another highly adaptable strategy that can be orchestrated to meet any number of standards. For example, say you want your adolescent writers to practice meeting this standard: "Develop the topic thoroughly by selecting the most significant and relevant facts, extended definitions, concrete details, quotations, or other information and examples appropriate to the audience's knowledge of the topic" (CCSS. ELA-Literacy.11-12.2.C).

One way to begin meeting this standard is to have adolescent writers practice developing a topic by selecting relevant quotations. If the topic of study revolves around an essential question such as "What are some sustainable solutions to environmental problems in our neighborhood?," a Board Races list of writing tasks could include the following:

1. Define "sustainable."
2. Write out a quotation from the readings relating to sustainability.
3. Name an environmental problem.
4. Write out a quotation from the readings to illustrate this environmental problem.

5. Write out three challenges to enacting sustainable solutions to environmental problems.
6. Write out a quotation illustrating one of these challenges.

Essay Jumble is a strategy explicitly teaching organization. As a result, this strategy is ideal for: "Organize complex ideas, concepts, and information so that each new element builds on that which precedes it to create a unified whole" (CCSS.ELA-Literacy.WHST.11-12.2.A).

Class Collection and *Class Newspaper* are two writing strategies particularly suited for digital production and publication as these compositions should be shared with a wide audience. As a result they are well suited for this Common Core writing standard: "Use technology, including the Internet, to produce, publish, and update individual or shared writing products in response to ongoing feedback, including new arguments or information" (CCSS.ELA-Literacy.WHST.11-12.6).

Finally, the notion of *All Writing Is Story* supports this Common Core articulation of narrative: "The Standards require that students be able to incorporate narrative elements effectively into arguments and informative/explanatory texts. In history/social studies, students must be able to incorporate narrative accounts into their analyses of individuals or events of historical import. In science and technical subjects, students must be able to write precise enough descriptions of the step-by-step procedures they use in their investigations or technical work that others can replicate them and (possibly) reach the same results" (from the Note section of English Language Arts Standards, Writing, Grade 11–12).

WHERE WE'VE BEEN AND WHERE WE'RE GOING

Based on brain science and testimonies from writer-teachers, this chapter places a premium on the purposeful development of positive affect when teaching writing to adolescent learners. Activities and frameworks are presented to facilitate vacillation between focused and defocused creative thinking, promote positive engagement, emphasize producing and creating, and communication with authentic audiences.

The overall message of this chapter is quite simple: Positive affect leads to better cognition, better writing. If we want our adolescent learners to be lifelong writers then we ought to make writing an enjoyable experience.

The next chapter, *Nonconscious Cognition and Writing*, makes the argument that the majority of our cognitive processes are in fact nonconscious. As a result, we must begin to understand what these nonconscious processes are, how they operate, how they develop, and how they impact writing and the teaching of writing. Several habits of mind with accompanying strategies are offered to support adolescent writers.

6

✛

Nonconscious Cognition and Writing

INTRODUCTION AND CHAPTER OVERVIEW

Nonconscious cognition is mental work completed outside of conscious awareness and is alternatively called implicit, bottom-up, unplanned, or unconscious. Nonconscious cognition is a sophisticated set of mental processes that occur largely without our awareness. In other words, our brains have evolved to do a lot of our thinking on autopilot, without recourse to conscious intent.

There are a few contextual facts to note about nonconscious cognition. First, nonconscious cognition makes up the majority of our mental work. Freud's view of consciousness as the tip of the iceberg was surprisingly conservative, as contemporary research on cognition reveals consciousness as but a snowball on the tip of that iceberg (Wilson, 2002, 6).

Nonconscious cognition is not a single mental function but, rather, a collection of mental functions. What this means for the teaching of writing is substantial as nonconscious cognition proves to be vital for both the struggling and accomplished writer at every stage of the writing process.

Nonconscious cognition is right at the borderlands of what we know and do not know about the brain and learning. While we do know nonconscious cognition is very real phenomena implicated in writing, there is less certainty about how nonconscious cognition operates within the learning and writing process.

Teaching and learning about nonconscious cognition takes us into an uncomfortable space because even as we recognize it as instructional time wisely spent we also know nonconscious cognition remains largely invisible to state and federal mandates and accompanying standards and assessments. Its contours are difficult to discern as nonconscious cognition stubbornly eludes the narrow confines of standardized testing and remains largely unquantifiable. Nevertheless, if its prevalence in brain science and writer-teacher testimonies are any indication of its significance, it is a space that should be fought for by teachers to be included in curricula.

This chapter will present evidence of nonconscious cognition from the brain sciences before sharing evidence from the testimonies of accomplished writer-teachers. In the usual manner, this chapter will include strategies to emphasize nonconscious cognition in the teaching of writing.

BRAIN SCIENCE AND NONCONSCIOUS COGNITION

There are a number of studies from brain science illustrating nonconscious cognition but perhaps none more famous than the case of Henry Molaison. In 1933, at seven years old, Molaison was struck and knocked unconscious by a bicyclist. For the next twenty years he suffered persistent, debilitating seizures until an operation removed parts of his hippocampus and amygdala. The operation controlled the seizures but unintentionally stripped Molaison of his ability to form new memories.

If you were to meet Henry Molaison, entering the room and shaking his hand, he could talk to you and appear completely normal. In fact, you would notice nothing out of the ordinary until, say, you left the room and came back. Upon your return he would have no memory of having met you even if you had been gone for just a few minutes.

Molaison's ability to form new memories was thought to be completely lost until Brenda Milner, a psychologist who worked with him soon after his surgery and for several years thereafter, discovered something extraordinary. In testing his memory Milner had him complete a mirror-tracing activity. The task for Molaison was to trace a five-pointed star, the difficulty being that he could only see the star as reflected in a mirror.

As Milner explains, "Under these conditions, we all tend to move the hand in the wrong direction when we reach the points of the star, but we gradually improve with practice over many trials." What is remarkable is that Molaison shows improvement in this activity along "a typical learning curve" even though "at the end of the last trial, he had absolutely no idea that he had ever done the task before." As Milner characterizes it, "This was learning without any sense of familiarity" (1998, 288).

The case of Henry Molaison, along with subsequently studied cases of amnesiacs, demonstrates that our brains have different modes of cognition with the most broad strokes delineating conscious and nonconscious cognitive faculties. As a direct result of Brenda Milner's work with Henry Molaison, one cannot open a psychology or neuroscience textbook today without encountering a diagram that immediately divides memory into two categories alternatively labeled as conscious/nonconscious, implicit/ explicit, or declarative/nondeclarative.

Antonio Damasio is a neuroscientist who provides another example of nonconscious cognition at work. Damasio argues that "Emotions are not a luxury" and are in fact essential for "cognitive guidance" (1994, 130). In the face of intricate and irreducibly complex processes such as writing, emotions play a pivotal role as they create hierarchies and strengthen representations in the mind of what is important for consideration and inclusion.

Damasio shares a story to illustrate what happens when emotion is taken out of the cognitive equation. One of his patients, suffering from ventromedial prefrontal damage, lacked the ability to use emotion to create cognitive hierarchies. In other words, this patient looked upon the world with reason and intellect alone, unable to draw from emotional markers to help facilitate complex decision making. Damasio, upon presenting two possible dates for the patient to return to the laboratory, relates how the patient:

> pulled out his appointment book and began consulting the calendar. The behavior that ensued, which was witnessed by several investigators, was remarkable. For the better part of a half-hour, the patient enumerated reasons for and against each of the two dates: previous engagements, proximity to other engagements, possible meteorological conditions, virtually anything that one could reasonably think about concerning a simple date. (193)

This experience finely illustrates the limitations of strict reason. Conscious knowledge is not enough—the brain relies heavily on nonconscious cognition in the form of intuition and emotions to help guide complex decision making. Without emotionally integrated feelings in the form of intuition and somatic markers the most simple of tasks derail into timeless exercises of cost-benefit analyses.

Another famous and fascinating case is the story of Solomon Shereshevsky. In the 1920s Shereshevsky was working as a newspaper reporter. As was customary, one early morning the editor gathered his group of reporters and related an extensive list of instructions including the names of several people to be interviewed along with addresses of their possible locations. While the group of reporters scratched furiously in their notepads as he spoke, the editor noticed that Shereshevsky had not written down a single instruction.

As a form of public reprimand the editor asked Shereshevsky to repeat the instructions. To everyone's surprise Shereshevsky was able to repeat the instructions verbatim. In time the editor advised him to visit a psychological laboratory to ascertain the extent of his memory. At the laboratory Shereshevsky met the neuropsychologist Alexander Luria. "This is how our acquaintance began," writes Luria, "which lasted for almost thirty years, filled with tests, conversations, and letters" (1987).

What becomes most interesting are the inherent limitations of Shereshevsky's infallible memory. For example, Shereshevsky had a very difficult time registering faces since they were always changing with age and emotive context:

> They're so changeable. A person's expression depends on his mood and on the circumstances under which you happen to meet him. People's faces are constantly changing; it's the different shades of expression that confuse me and make it so hard to remember faces.

This difficulty recognizing and remembering faces was indicative of a larger cognitive deficit relating to abstract concepts and figurative language. The power of his memory drowned his perception in details to such an extent that he was to describe the reading of a story as "all the details that have nothing to do with the task . . . and I cannot hold on to the main idea."

What brain science has come to understand about the function of the brain from cases such as Solomon Shereshevsky and Henry Molaison is that conscious knowledge has its limits and that nonconscious cognitive processes in the form of intuition and emotions work in concert with consciousness to enable and guide complex decision making.

As will be made clear from the testimonies of writer-teachers, this mixture of conscious and nonconscious cognition is very much at the heart of the writing process. Before getting to the testimonies from writer-teachers, there are two more relevant findings from brain science related to nonconscious cognition to introduce: the default mode network and the role of sleep.

Like many scientific discoveries, the default mode network was discovered by accident. Brain imaging studies utilizing fMRI technology burst onto the scene and proliferated in the 1990s leading many to dub the 1990s as "the decade of the brain." Most brain imaging studies were organized in similar fashion. A participant would be placed into a scanner and asked to do a mental activity such as read a word, solve a mathematical problem, view an image. In order to pinpoint parts of the brain being employed to complete the directed mental activity, brain scientists would utilize a passive activity to serve as a baseline. Passive activities took the form of participants being asked to focus on a crosshair or simply being instructed to rest between directed activities.

Brain scientists conducting these experiments were, of course, interested in the images they were receiving while the participants were performing the directed task. It took several years for scientists to begin realizing that the passive activity showed similar brain activity across a wide range of participants within these studies. Gradually brain scientists began to realize that the passive activities—the times when participants were simply instructed to rest or defocus—showed networked, spontaneous activity in the brain.

This discovery of the default mode network—what we experience daily as daydreaming, stream-of-conscious thought, or stimulus-independent thought—was a paradigmatic shift in brain science. Once scientists began to study the default mode network purposefully they made several discoveries. The default mode network is a set of connected networks in the brain comprised primarily of the prefrontal cortex, medial parietal cortex, and the medial temporal lobes (see figure 6.1).

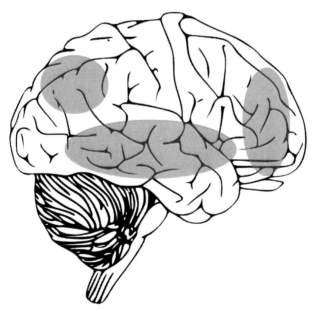

Figure 6.1. Interconnected network of the default mode network including the prefrontal cortex, medial parietal cortex, and medial temporal lobes.

These brain regions, working in a coordinated effort when we go "off-line" into nonconscious states of daydreaming and stimulus-independent thought happen to be the newest parts of our brains from an evolutionary standpoint. It appears the default mode network is a rather recent evolutionary step and one that scientists argue is as important as the development of language.

The default mode network, in essence, allows "the construction of mental modes or simulations that are adaptive and facilitate future behavior" (Buckner, 2012, 6). (As can be imagined, similar brain structures are called into action when completing Theory of Mind activities, discussed in chapter 2.)

Lending further validity and insight to the default mode network is the fact that various cognitive disorders such as ADHD, Alzheimer's, schizophrenia, depression, and autism demonstrate abnormalities in the default mode network. Additionally, the default mode network shows greater myelination from childhood to adulthood and is a network largely unique to humans. In sum, the daydreaming, "off-line," nonconscious cognition associated with the default mode network is anything but wasted time as it plays an essential role in human living from basic survival on up to creative endeavors such as writing.

The final mode of nonconscious cognition to examine is the most easily identifiable: sleep. It is well documented that sleep plays an important role before and after learning. Sleep prepares the brain to learn. Sleep deprivation induces negative cognitive states, including declines in focus, judgment, and muscle coordination, which can lead to injury. Neurons become overburdened and lose their ability to coordinate new information and recall previously learned information. Lack of and low-quality sleep also negatively impact mood—an important element of writing discussed in chapter 5, *Positive Affect and Writing*.

Sleep also plays a principal role after learning. Sleep has evolved to help consolidate different types of memories such as declarative and procedural. Robert Stickgold, a preeminent sleep researcher, has found that different stages of sleep help to consolidate different types of memories. During sleep the brain works to get faster and more efficient at learned processes as well as find new ways to carry out tasks.

Sleep also consolidates memories by strengthening, stabilizing, maintaining, and integrating them in the brain. Sleep can also help us to understand rules and realize creative insights. Stickgold (2014) concludes: "Cognition outside of attention, whether in wake or sleep and whether conscious or nonconscious, facilitates what may well be the most sophisticated functions that the human brain performs—building a model of our world, creating the meaning within our lives and writing the stories of our literature."

WRITER-TEACHERS SPEAK TO NONCONSCIOUS COGNITION

Popular brain scientist Antonio Damasio supports bringing together brain science with the humanities to help us further understand creative pursuits such as writing. Damasio envisions "a two-way bridge could be established between neurobiology and the humanities" that could ultimately provide "for a more comprehensive account of creativity" (1994, xiv). We have already traversed the bridge of nonconscious cognition from the scientific side; this section will construct the bridge from the side of writer-teachers.

Writer-teachers consistently reference aspects of the writing process they do not understand yet trust and rely on. A sampling from the interviews with writer-teachers helps to begin illustrating this phenomenon:

> It's something I know and can't say. (James Gee)
> I don't know what the dynamics of it are. (Mike Rose)
> I used to think invention was more explicitly controllable. I don't think
>   that anymore. (Julie Lindquist)
> I can't explain it. (Mariah Fredericks)
> I don't know what my brain does. (Simone White)

To organize the ways in which these writer-teachers speak to nonconscious cognition, three sets of commonly deployed metaphors will be investigated. These resonant metaphorical sets are: (1) Discovery, Surprise, Fresh Eyes; (2) Deferring, Not Knowing, DNA; and (3) Mixing, Balancing, Perfect Ratio.

Discovery, Surprise, Fresh Eyes

Brenda Greene says she writes, "To find out what I really know, I think that as a writer I wind up always doing journaling and write to figure out what I really, really think. It forces me to slow down and to reflect and to really go deep down and to try and understand what it is that I've gained." In emphasizing writing to "understand what it is that I've gained," Greene is positioning writing as a process of discovery.

Writers purposefully look to be surprised by their writing. Successful transference, wherein implicit knowledge breaks through to explicit language, is accompanied by a feeling of surprise and this feeling is a primary reason writers keep returning to the difficult process of writing. There is something inherently pleasurable about being surprised. Pulitzer Prize winner Yusef Komunyakaa speaks to the joy of surprise and its centrality to the invention process:

> If the poem is a template of what we already know, it doesn't surprise us. I think that's why artists do what they do—they want to be surprised, they want to be able to laugh. I love where there's a moment when I'm laughing and I think, "Oh gosh, where did that come from?" because it surprised me. "Gosh, I really didn't intend to say that that particular way but it surprised me."

Peter Elbow calls this surprise the "deepest pleasure" in writing. "It's in there and you didn't know it's in there," he says. "The figuring out often involves discovery and new thoughts."

Nancy Sommers speaks to this phenomenon as well, saying, "You want to be surprised." It follows that truly inventive writing, writing that is indeed novel to the writer, will be experienced as surprise. These feelings of surprise are also the most enjoyable moments for these writers. Sommers says, "I just love those surprises. I love the surprise of putting down the words and just being blown away by the swoon of the word and then that whole surprise of reading, reading, reading, and letting the writing tell me what it wants to say, and then feeling that each time I come back to it, it tells a different story." These are the moments that keep writers circling back to the blank page.

Art Markman and Mike Rose independently spoke to the importance of reading with "fresh eyes." In the case of Markman, he references one of the benefits of working with a book-length project as "by the time you get to the end it's been so long since you read the beginning that you've forgotten most of what you wrote in its details which means you can read it again with fresher eyes." This is to gain benefits from the distance that a lapse in time affords, the benefits from a period of incubation. Mike Rose speaks similarly to this experience of incubation:

> That's a phenomenon that I know you're familiar with and that so many people have written about and it's still a bit mysterious and that's where you work and work and work on something and you just hit an endpoint and often you feel like it wasn't very productive or you feel stymied and then you come back to it the next day, or you come back to it later, and it falls into place. . . . It's wild. They call it incubation in the creativity literature but that is an actual phenomenon. I don't know what the dynamics of it are but, boy, it sure is true. And so this thing that I was talking about of being away from it for the day and then coming back to it and it's late at night—you can kind of return to the thing with fresh eyes.

The metaphor provided by Markman and Rose of fresh eyes is the experience of capitalizing on the work the nonconscious mind has done during a time of incubation.

Deferring, Not Knowing, DNA

It may appear counterintuitive but knowing too much about the writing can actually be limiting. There are various ways of knowing, and to jump to the most readily available and dominant, not to mention the new kid on the evolutionary block in terms of brain development—consciousness—is to close off other ways of knowing such as those as afforded by nonconscious cognition.

Yusef Komunyakaa says, "I am less positive about the progress of the piece if I already know too much beforehand." Andrea Lunsford reflects, "I do take a rational approach to writing, but not exclusively rational because I think we're learning that our emotions are involved in everything we do and everything we think." Elizabeth Nunez says, "I can't say I planned it; it just happened." William Olsen offers a detailed vision of nonconscious cognition. After saying, "I think good work has to trust to the unknown," Olsen explains:

> The instant I hear a student saying, "I wanted the poem to do this," I instantly distrust the poem. My guess is that the poem has been overconsciously directed towards event. I think that in revising in a certain sense you want not to apprehend where you are going and not to understand the poem for as long as possible because the instant you understand it you reduce the poem to the lowest level of your understanding. In fact, I don't think a poem is done until its ending in a way defies, even if it encourages, paraphrase. . . . Let me say that differently. If the end of the poem I write exceeds my understanding, I know maybe it's worth staying with. Ultimately the end product has to outstrip an individual understanding, an individual consciousness.

Purposefully deferring conscious understanding is an intellectual stance wherein writers trust to the unknown, allowing the characters or the data or the "whatever" to take over. It's an intellectual position of "figuring out how to get out of the way" (Olsen), recognizing that writing has potential to outsmart the writer. There is a commitment to the work, which supersedes the writer's individual awareness.

Stuart Dybek describes this commitment as "a kind of relationship" continuing, "rather than looking to dominate this piece with a previous agenda what I'm looking to do is have this relationship with stuff that's already written that I'm going to surrender to, or that is going to prompt from me something I wouldn't ordinarily have written."

Implicit, nonconscious invention is not restricted to those working within creative genres. Academic writer Peter Elbow, for example, champions the unplanned: "It's so amazing that nonplanning is such a source of creativity and richness and even clarity." Nancy Sommers agrees, saying, "You don't want to impose your ideas or opinions on the data. The data has to speak and reveal itself, or the sources, and that's what I was trying very much to do, was to learn from it rather than impose some way of seeing upon it."

Writers understand or intuit consciousness as a gluttonous mechanism insisting on understanding. Fighting this impulse toward reductionism requires a relinquishing of control. Yusef Komunyakaa says, "You have some control but you don't have ultimate control. One has the illusion that he or she has control. We don't need that control," concluding, "I do think that mystery should remain in the poem."

Gene Yang says, "I almost feel like the creative process, you have to lose a little bit of control over the creative process in order for your project to have a life. If your project has a life of its own you're going to, it'll almost feel like it's making its own decisions at some point." This notion of allowing the writing "a life of its own" is repeated by these writer-teachers as a DNA metaphor, here articulated by Peter Elbow:

> The thought knows where it wants to go. I mean, I have to stand out of the way and let that thought, free write and let that thought go where it wants to go. Let it go where it wants to go. It'll go somewhere. It has, it knows where it wants to go. . . . It has the DNA seed in it.

Patrick Bizzaro speaks in similar terms to this DNA metaphor: "I follow it wherever it seems to want to go. I don't always know for sure. But I swear that the subject insists upon a genre." Playwright Richard Maxwell is thankful that the writing is independent of the writer as this frees him from being solely responsible for the work:

> I'm also relieved that it's not based on my ego. I mean, of course, I wrote and directed the thing, but it's like once the thing [is produced], it can never, you can't steer it. You just can't. No matter how much control you think you have over something, you can never steer it, and I wouldn't want to because then you kind of kill it. So the thing is, it's like a beast.

These testimonies reference moments of nonconscious cognition, of trusting the writing to lead the writer as if the writing itself contains its own heartbeat distinct from that of its author.

Mixing, Balancing, Perfect Ratio

The final view of writer-teachers utilizing nonconscious cognition is one of the writer effortlessly dipping in and out of these metaphorical categories with such speed that the categories seemingly dissolve. This is to view the boundaries between these metaphors, as well as the boundaries between conscious and nonconscious thought, as beneficially permeable.

Nancy Sommers sums it up well: "The more, I think, a confident, sophisticated mature writer you are, everything gets so mixed up that it's hard to be able to identify a distinct phase, the revision phase, the invention phase. It gets so intertwined." Elizabeth Nunez states succinctly, "I write with a conscious self and an unconscious self, and they must coexist." William Olsen offers a detailed view of vacillating between the nonconscious (he calls it the unconscious) and conscious during the invention process:

> I have to get the unconscious kicked in just to generate stuff, and the way I do it, as I said earlier, is to read first. That makes it possible for me to read with a little less ego involved, with less expectations, and less self-conscious. Maybe that makes the unconscious come to play more readily. Then I have to examine what I've said and read it because the unconscious is more than capable of throwing out clichés. Then, when I've done that, I have to allow the unconscious to come back into play again. (Olsen)

Elizabeth Nunez and Robert Stickgold offer metaphors to explain the interstitial nature of conscious and nonconscious processes in writing. Nunez says, "I think of it as a jockey on a horse, you know, and that's the unconscious self knowing. You believe in it, and if you hold the reins too much, it's not going to win the race. On the other hand, if you let it go, it's not going to win the race either. So it's a balancing act."

Stickgold refers to writing as "a combination of top-down and bottom-up processes," explaining further, "You go through a series of practices, physical and mental, that help you get into a particular mental state. And that's a mental state where those top-down and bottom-up processes are both activated in the quote 'perfect ratio.'" The mixing, balancing, perfect ratio metaphor is all about nonconscious and conscious cognitive faculties working in such close proximity that they become usefully indistinguishable.

NONCONSCIOUS COGNITION AND TEACHING WRITING

Since nonconscious cognition is by nature a rather elusive concept it is more difficult to translate directly into writing strategies and activities. It becomes more suitable and practical to think along the lines of habits of mind or dispositions toward the writing process in order to capitalize on nonconscious cognition.

This section will present three dispositions toward writing drawn from brain science and writer-teacher testimonies alongside suggested activities. The three dispositions are (1) Writing as Discovery; (2) The Usefulness of Not Knowing; and (3) Balancing the Conscious and Nonconscious.

Writing as Discovery

Stuart Dybek shares, "If you regard writing as discovery what you try to do frequently is place yourself in a situation where you don't know where you are going." Writing without knowing where you are going to end up, without an a priori game plan or thesis in mind, is the essence of writing to discover. Dybek continues, "You want accidents to happen. You can't create the accident, but you're hoping to create the condition that might create the accident."

What are some conditions "that might create the accident" for adolecent writers? In other words, what are some writing activities that help adolescent writers discover what they do not know? The following activities are designed to place adolescent writers into a space in which they are writing to discover.

- *Freewriting.* This strategy is first introduced in chapter 2, *Theory of Mind and Writing,* but is worth recalling here. Freewriting—writing continuously for a set period of time in a stream-of-consciousness fashion—is a wonderful strategy to help adolescents write themselves into new thoughts and understandings.

Peter Elbow is a writer-teacher who has championed freewriting for decades. He describes freewriting as "a machine . . . for producing non-planned work and nonplanned thought." In this manner freewriting makes explicit in language what begins as implicit, nonconscious thought.

- *Journey of the Imagination.* This activity is a personal favorite. The idea is to create a prompt in which adolescents first listen and then respond in writing—a prompt that asks them to take a journey using their imagination. First, have them put everything aside except for a piece of paper and a writing instrument. Then go over the rules: There can be absolutely no talking during this exercise as talking will disrupt the thoughts and thus imaginative journey of others. Consider turning off some of the lights and asking adolescents to close their eyes. I usually begin with a warm-up activity to help get the adolescent writers acclimated to the activity. The warm-up consists of the following prompt:

Journey of the Imagination Warm-Up Prompt
When you are comfortable close your eyes and place your writing hand on top of the desk in front of you with your palm facing up. Imagine there is a pen resting in your palm. It can be a pen that you know or a completely imaginary pen, one that you've never seen before. What are its distinguishing features? Is there anything written on the pen, if so, what is written on

the pen? Is it a push-pen or does it have a cap or does it work some other way? Feel the weight of the pen in your hand. What would you compare the weight of the pen to? What color does the pen write? Imagine yourself writing a sentence with your pen. When you know what sentence it is that you write, open your eyes and write this sentence along with an accurate description of the pen so that if someone were to read what you wrote they could see the pen you imagined.

After the warm-up I ask adolescents to share the one sentence they wrote down. This doesn't take much time and everyone can share their sentence or pass if they do not wish to share. A few adolescents may volunteer to read their descriptions and the question is always posed: "Did you imagine something that surprised you?" Most adolescents will have seen and written about something they did not anticipate.

The "main" prompt comes after the warm-up and can be tailored to course content. Here is a sample prompt for a Spanish-language classroom:

Journey of the Imagination: Spanish Language
Imagine yourself leaving this classroom, leaving this school, leaving this town, even leaving this country. Pick a Spanish-speaking country you would like to visit. You are now in your chosen destination. Look around you. What do you see? What do you see in front of you, behind you? What type of ground is at your feet? Inhale through your nose, what do you smell? If you had to describe what you smell as taste, what would that taste be? What time of day is it? What is the weather like? How do you feel about being in this location? Are you happy, calm, sad, excited, something else? Listen closely to the sounds around you. What do you hear? Imagine that someone is with you in this place. It can be a friend who travelled with you or a stranger you have just met. Imagine you are talking with this person in Spanish. What are you talking about? What are you saying? After you imagine a few lines of dialogue, open your eyes and write down this dialogue along with an accurate description of this place so that if someone were to read what you wrote, they would have this experience of being there.

Again, it's time well spent to allow adolescents time to write and then share their writing. As a sharing strategy for this prompt have the adolescents name the location they visited and a line of dialogue from their visit. Then adolescents can share what they have written in small groups before electing someone from their group to share with the whole class.

This activity invariably triggers a number of surprises for the adolescent writers. Often they had never been to the place they imagined nor did they anticipate the events experienced on their journeys. This writing activity never fails to serve as a bridge between implicit nonconscious thought and explicit conscious, descriptive writing. As a bonus, adolescents enjoy this activity; it's an activity that stimulates positive affect.

- *Adopting a New Voice.* Ask adolescents to experiment with writing in a new voice, a voice that is distinctly not their own, a voice that they can write inside of without knowing what's going to come out. This voice can be any number of archetypes such as the overconfident fool, the wise old man, the self-conscious teenager, etc. This voice can also come from course reading materials—a main or peripheral character or historical person.

The emphasis here should be placed on letting the adopted voice lead the narration so the writing is being discovered as it is being composed. Robert Stickgold speaks to this process:

> I would literally just imagine the conversations and type them out. And in those cases, I don't know what different people are going to say in that conversation ahead of time, and I don't feel like I often make a conscious decision that this is what the person should say. All of a sudden, a character says, "Well, that's really stupid, I can't believe you said that," and if that's what the character says, that's what I type. So I think there's a lot of associative processing and language construction that, as an author, I will allow to happen outside of my control and awareness.

- *Emotional Register.* Sondra Perl references this generative habit of mind (she names it "felt sense") as she speaks in detail to adopting an attentive stance, waiting for the emergence of nonconscious thought to transfer into writing:

> There's a kind of attentiveness, just waiting for a nibble or, you know, it's a kind of patience. . . . I'm waiting for it to emerge. It's going from what is implicit and I would say locatable in the body to what is explicit in language. And so what is implicitly happening experientially is a bodily sense of—you don't have the words yet. You're waiting for those words to come. But if you turn your attention inward and try to cultivate what is—what am I sensing, what am I feeling? Not quite feeling like am I hungry or angry but just what's there? And you absolutely have to pause and be quiet, words will come or an image will come or a phrase will come.

Perl characterizes this intellectual position as getting "below the conscious-conscious mind." The writer's goal within this state of invention is to discover what the nonconscious already knows. Using one's emotional register links to the emotional state of knowing that Antonio Damasio features in his brain science studies.

Registering emotions is all about (1) understanding emotions as indicators of nonconscious cognition and (2) improving the writer's ability to register these emotional indicators. Some questions to facilitate this process include:

- How am I feeling about the writing? Proud? Embarrassed? Excited? Bored? What are some ways to improve my reaction to my writing?
- Is there a central image or idea guiding the writing? What is it?
- What is my gut reaction to the writing?
- Am I enjoying the writing process? What are my favorite parts of writing? What are my least favorite parts of writing and what would improve my attitude?
- What's not in the writing yet that needs to be? Where does the writing seem to be going?

Registering emotions can be particularly effective when revising. Elizabeth Kerlikowske relates how, upon receiving the proofs for a publication, she asked the editor to take out a few lines because when she read the lines she felt "physically sick" as if it were "a cloud that passes over." This attunement to her emotional register guides her revision process.

The Usefulness of Not Knowing

It is counterintuitive but nonetheless commonly accepted among teacher-writers that too much conscious knowledge can be a bad thing for the writing process. Too much conscious knowledge means the writer has placed herself squarely in the mode of using writing to present preconceived beliefs as opposed to using writing to discover new learning.

We have already heard from Yusef Komunyakaa, who says, "I am less positive about the progress of the piece if I already know too much beforehand," and William Olsen who distrusts student intentionality in writing. The driving idea behind this section, "The Usefulness of Not Knowing," is that adolescents should be encouraged and challenged to write themselves right off the cliff and into the unknown. Strategies for doing so include:

- *Begin with an Unanswered Question.* If you really want your adolescent writers to be using writing as a tool for discovery, then the question driving their writing should not be immediately answerable. If an adolescent writer can answer the question behind her writing at the beginning of the writing process then the writing is more presentation than discovery. Of course there should be a time when the adolescent writer can articulate an answer, but this should be at a far remove from the start of the writing process.

The unanswered question driving the writing should also evolve over time in response to research conducted, readings analyzed, and writing completed. Formulating and reformulating unanswered questions is a skill that adolescent writers benefit from practicing.

Questions guiding research and writing should also be, first and foremost, engaging to the writer and, secondly, to potential readers. Finding the balance between questions that are far too broad (i.e., too many subordinate questions associated with it) or far too narrow (i.e., too easily answered in the affirmative or positive without much nuance or development required) needs to be taught explicitly. Table 6.1 clarifies for adolescent writers the scope a particular research report should take.

Table 6.1.

Too Broad	Too Narrow	Just Right
What makes a good test taker?	What are three strategies for taking a standardized test?	What are the strategies enacted by effective standardized test takers before, during, and after a test session?
What are the benefits and disadvantages of being bicultural?	What is the definition of bicultural?	What is the experience of being exceptionally bicultural like?
What are the personality traits of introverts?	How are extroverts and introverts defined?	What are some advantages of being an introvert in a society that favors extroverts?

This chart is meant to be adapted and can be used to clarify for adolescent writers the appropriate depth and breadth of unanswered questions for any number of writing assignments. Here is an adolescent writer's introductory paragraph utilizing one of the unanswered questions posed above:

In the United States it is normal "to be from somewhere else." Oftentimes natives are the real rarity. The nature of these cultural hybrids stretch from people who live in bubbles of their native lands, barely interacting with anyone outside of their own culture, to people so well acclimated that their first culture and language are left in the past, barely a force in everyday life. But what about the people who seem to be always in both cultures and languages, in ways constantly toggling back and forth, people who seem to be as American as they are of another place? What is this experience of being exceptionally bicultural like?

Composing unanswered questions to guide the research and writing process is also a means of deferring interpretive closure. Rather than opting for quick closure on complex topics, composing and recomposing unanswered questions helps to extend and deepen the development of one's topic.

- *The Combinatorial Power of Writing.* This strategy highlights the usefulness of not knowing by pushing adolescent writers into a third, unpredictable space. The concept is simple: image/idea + image/idea = unpredictable combination.

What happens when we bring together a brick wall with a spider? An apron with snow? A refrigerator with an old man? Challenge adolescent writers to add two familiar images together to create an unpredictable combination.

The same equation works when we replace the images with ideas: What happens when we bring together the idea of free will with space exploration? Global warming with animal rights? Educational curriculum with the role of athletes? Combining two familiar ideas together leads adolescents into a third, unpredictable space in their writing.

This activity is easily adapted to class concepts. As an example, figure 6.2 lists a number of concepts related to a unit on gravitational forces and densities. Adolescents are asked to combine two or more of these unit concepts in their writing.

Atmosphere	Density	Humidity	Wind Belts
Jet Stream	Ocean Current	Coriolis Effect	Heat Transfer
Precipitation	Evaporation	Boundary Currents	Gravity
Temperature	Earth's Rotation	Wind Current	
Atmospheric Circulation	Gravitational Force	Salinity	Climate

Figure 6.2.

- *Writing into and out of Tough Situations.* This strategy encourages adolescent writers to push themselves into new territory by writing themselves into and out of a tough situation. Gene Yang describes this strategy, which he learned from his own writing mentor who was a writer for the G.I. Joe television series: "He would come up with some scenario, some deadly scenario . . . and the scenario had to be complex enough that he couldn't think of a solution right way." Yang concludes, "I think that's a great way of approaching a story, the idea of coming up with a problem that has a very, very difficult solution, and then the writing process is basically the solution process."

This strategy of creating a tough situation and then writing one's way out of it works for more than just storytelling genres. In a history class, for example, adolescent writers could be given the following prompt: "Suddenly you find yourself in front of a tour group at Stonehenge. You are asked to explain why it was built. What do you say?" And here is a tough situational prompt for a mathematics classroom: "Calculus was not discovered until the late 1600s by Isaac Newton and Gottfried Leibniz (the two argued over who discovered it first), well after many colleges had been founded. Explain the purpose and importance of calculus to someone who has never heard of it before."

Adolescents can also create their own tough situations to challenge their writing prowess. Another adaptation of this strategy has adolescents creating tough scenarios to share and to challenge classmates to write out possible solutions.

Balancing the Conscious and Nonconscious

The final dispositional view to impart here for the teaching of writing is to view conscious and nonconscious cognition as having evolved to support one another. This holistic view of writing posits that the mature, sophisticated writer is marked by an ability to transfer quickly and successfully between conscious and nonconscious processes.

This section will introduce this dual-process model of writing before speaking to incubation—a central component of writing and one that highlights the integration of conscious and nonconscious cognition.

- *Dual-Process Model of Writing.* This model of the writing process introduced by David Galbraith (1999) brings together the knowledge-constituting model of writing with the problem-solving model of writing. In sum, knowledge-constituting strategies seek to create new knowledge while problem-solving strategies seek to analyze and organize existing knowledge and data. Table 6.2 displays a few

Table 6.2.

Knowledge-Constituting Model	Problem-Solving Model
Writing To Learn (WTL)	Writing To Show Learning (WTSL)
Creator	Editor
Receptivity	Discernment
Audience as Self	Audience as Readers
Writing to Discover	Writing as Presentation
Incubation	Deliberate Practice

concepts introduced in this book and how they fit into this dual-process model.

Several dualities can be added to this table but the greater point is that the successful writer vacillates effectively between these two states of mind. The knowledge-constituting model is represented by strategies to mine the nonconscious. Cognitive gains completed outside of conscious awareness can be made explicit through knowledge-constituting strategies. A wonderfully illustrative example of this process is incubation.

- *Incubation.* A process every writer values, incubation is an indispensible strategy to any classroom focused on writing instruction. Incubation refers to the benefits accrued by nonconscious cognition while the brain is no longer consciously engaged in writing. Incubation is the time between conscious efforts at writing. This promotes the ability to see one's writing with "fresh eyes" as both Mike Rose and Art Markman attest.

Incubation is paired with brain science concepts of the default mode network and sleep. The default mode network is the productive state our brains enter when not consciously engaged in a task (i.e., while mind wandering). How does this relate to the teaching of writing? Adolescent writers should become purposeful about structuring periods of incubation as part of their writing routines.

Entering into the default mode network, or mind wandering, is unavoidable; we are, in fact, biologically engineered mind wanderers. Being purposeful about such mind wandering is a crucial strategy. Adolescents can learn to productively vacillate between deliberate, conscious writing states and default mode network states. One way to enable a productive routine is by keeping a Writer's Log where adolescents track the time spent on-task and time spent off-task. Having a plan for the time spent not writing can improve the overall writing experience and the writing itself.

As evinced from brain science, sleep is invaluable to learning. Writer-teachers speak to the connections between sleep and writing. Yusef Komunyakaa, for example, makes the case for keeping a notebook close at hand where one sleeps: "I started writing everything down, especially right before I go to sleep because a phrase can sort of enter one's psyche and disturb, I think, the sleep pattern. It's waiting to get out, it's waiting for you to open your eyes and of course it's all subconscious."

Adam Higginbotham says, "You're better able to take in information after you've slept properly," and George Irish shares an anecdote demonstrating the ability of sleep to conduct cognition outside conscious awareness:

> I remember in high school when I had a math problem I couldn't solve I would just go to bed and wake up at midnight and the solution would be there as if it were written on the wall. Sometimes because your body is so tired your mind just can't focus. Tiredness can be a distraction. I have found sleep to be a very useful companion; it certainly helps me with my writing.

The takeaway for the writing classroom is that adolescents need both quality and quantity when it comes to sleep if they are going to function well in a learning environment. While there are no guaranteed ways of ensuring adolescents get the quality and quantity of sleep they need, making adolescents, parents, teachers, and administrators aware of sleep's importance to their learning and ongoing brain development is a good first step. Asking adolescents to compare the quality of their thinking when well rested as opposed to exhausted is another way to feature the improved cognitive faculties afforded by sleep.

NONCONSCIOUS COGNITION AND WRITING: CONNECTIONS TO THE ENGLISH LANGUAGE ARTS WRITING COMMON CORE STATE STANDARDS

An ongoing concern with standards is the tendency to oversimplify complex processes. Take this standard from the Common Core as an example: "Produce clear and coherent writing in which the development, organization, and style are appropriate to task, purpose, and audience" (CCSS. ELA-Literacy.WHST.11-12.4).

Of course we all want this in our writing. Adolescent writers want this. Accomplished writer-teachers want this. Reflecting on our own writing process and talking with accomplished writer-teachers, however, illuminates how difficult and messy the process can be in order to achieve such "clear and coherent writing." Standards tend to make writing appear more consciously controllable and manageable than experience and practice demonstrates.

Another source of confusion for adolescent writers is how finished writing, especially in more academic genres, outwardly presents "clear and coherent writing" as if it came straight from the head of the author to the page. Accomplished writers know this not to be the case. The writing process is a messy, recursive experience marked by anything but linearity. Final refinement of ideas into their finished written form hides this story of messiness so effectively as to deceive adolescent writers into perceiving the writing process as fully governed by conscious intent.

An argument set forth by this chapter is that writing is an ideal tool to expand one's thinking, not simply reify what one already knows or believes about a given topic. *Writing to Discover* strategies such as *Freewriting, Journey of the Imagination, Adopt a New Voice, The Combinatorial Power of Writing*, and *Writing into and out of Tough Situations* seek to take the writer away from what is already consciously known and into new areas of thinking and writing.

There are several contact points between the CCSS and the strategies presented in this chapter on nonconscious cognition and writing. Writing to Discover, for example, connects with this standard: "Write informative/explanatory texts, including the narration of historical events, scientific procedures/experiments, or technical processes" (CCSS.ELA-Literacy.WHST.11-12.2).

The "narration of historical events" and the narration of "scientific procedures/experiments" and even "technical processes" are ripe moments to pursue writing to discover as adolescents narrate events as they unfold. This is writing into the unknown as adolescents record experiences while conducting an experiment or follow the narrative of a historical figure without knowing where the narration will take them.

The strategy of *Begin with an Unanswered Question* meets the call for "including self-generated questions." Refining these questions over the course of a writing project by choosing a question that is appropriate in terms of breadth and depth meets the CCSS call to "narrow or broaden the inquiry when appropriate" (CCSS.ELA-Literacy.WHST.11-12.7).

"Trying a new approach" (CCSS.ELA-Literacy.WHST.11-12.5) fits the type of dispositional thinking described in this chapter. Rather than staying with first impressions, adolescent writers should be encouraged to defer interpretive closure and think through the various approaches, or genres, that potentially best communicate their thinking.

"Use words, phrases, and clauses as well as varied syntax to link the major sections of the text, create cohesion, and clarify the relationships between claim(s) and reasons, between reasons and evidence, and between claim(s) and counterclaims" (CCSS.ELA-Literacy.WHST.11-12.1.C). Writing into the unknown goes hand in hand with trying out new and unfamiliar vocabulary, clauses, and syntactic elements as called for in this standard.

WHERE WE'VE BEEN AND WHERE WE'RE GOING

Nonconscious cognition references a wide-ranging set of cognitive faculties occurring outside of conscious awareness, cognitive faculties evolved to support complex decision making and creative pursuits such as writing. Brain science helps illustrate such nonconscious cognitive faculties as intuition, emotional registers, and the benefits afforded by the default mode network and sleep.

Testimonies from accomplished writer-teachers substantiate the importance of nonconscious cognition in the writing process. Writer-teachers speak in depth to habits of mind or dispositions toward writing in at least three ways: (1) treating the writing as a process of discovery; (2) valuing not knowing while writing and writing into the unknown; and (3) balancing nonconscious and conscious approaches during the writing process. Strategies for adolescent writers are offered alongside these habits of mind.

Bringing It All Together: The Metacognitive Writing Classroom is the next and final chapter. This concluding chapter brings together the central components of this book, arguing for a metacognitive writing classroom in which students and teachers alike are cognizant of the ways our brains interact with writing. This chapter focuses on strategies to help promote a metacognitive writing classroom in which brain science plays an inspirational and galvanizing role.

7

✝

Bringing It All Together: The Metacognitive Writing Classroom

INTRODUCTION AND CHAPTER OVERVIEW

Metacognition is literally translated as cognition about cognition. In other words, thinking about how we think. This entire book is essentially a practice in metacognition, a practice in thinking about our understandings of writing and writing instruction through the convergent lenses of brain science and writer-teacher testimonials.

Why should we think about how we think? What are the advantages of knowing how we think about writing and the teaching of writing? The answer to this question is that metacognitive awareness about writing and teaching writing stabilizes our understandings, improves performance, and facilitates transferability. Metacognition serves as the bridge between implicit nonconscious cognition and explicit conscious cognition.

To place this concluding chapter on metacognition within the broader context of this book, chapter 1, *Automaticity and Writing*, is about the purposeful development of nonconscious cognition in the form of habit, intuition, and craft. Automatizing elements of the writing process allows adolescent writers to reach higher and higher levels of cognition relevant to writing.

Chapter 6, *Nonconscious Cognition and Writing*, deals with valuing nonconscious cognition as it surfaces in various forms such as emotional markers, daydreaming, and sleep. This chapter on metacognition is about moving nonconscious, automatized ways of writing and thinking into consciousness where the nonconscious can be stabilized to improve performance and transferability.

106

F. Scott Fitzgerald famously wrote: "The test of a first-rate intelligence is the ability to hold two opposed ideas in mind at the same time and still retain the ability to function" (1936). Any complex endeavor is rife with paradox and even contradiction. This holds true with the teaching of writing.

While the notion of automaticity purports the benefits of moving conscious knowledge into an unconscious, automatized state, the notion of nonconscious cognition lauds the benefits of implicit knowledge, arguing that the writing process should not, nor can it ever, be completely rendered conscious. This chapter, in contrast, argues for the importance of metacognition—the movement of nonconscious cognition into consciousness.

Examples from brain science and testimonies from writer-teachers are offered to elucidate metacognition as a bridge between the unknown and known. Strategies designed to foster metacognition in adolescent writers are shared.

BRAIN SCIENCE AND METACOGNITION

Brain science provides wonderfully revealing studies to help explore metacognition. One of these studies is known as the eight-pair matching task. In this matching task eight pairs of items are set in front of a participant who is then asked to pick the "correct" item out of each pair. For example, you may be presented with a shoe and a coffee mug and asked to pick which item is correct. If you have done this task previously you will most likely remember the coffee mug as the correct item so you pick up the coffee mug and see that "correct" is written on its underside. Eight pairs of items are presented in this task with each item being marked as "correct" or "incorrect."

The insight for metacognition comes from noting how different test subjects perform on this task. For example, typical human subjects don't need more than one or two trials to begin performing at a very high rate of accuracy. Using conscious memorization, human test subjects remember which of the eight objects are the correct objects after just a few trials.

Monkeys, a closely related mammal sharing much of our brain anatomy, learn to complete the eight-pair matching task differently. The monkey learns the task as a gradually formed nonconscious habit over the course of around five hundred trials—a much different learning process than conscious memorization.

This eight-pair matching task gets even more interesting when administered to amnesiacs. Amnesiacs, remember, are patients with impaired short-term memory. Amnesiacs have access to long-term memories but have lost the ability to form new memories as a result of virus or, in the case of Henry Molaison, an operation to reduce the seizures in his brain. Amnesiacs learn to complete the eight-pair matching task in the same way as the monkeys—as a gradually developed habit over time.

So what does all this have to do with metacognition? Metacognition is an awareness of learning, something the monkeys and amnesiacs can't access during this task. To illustrate, one of the amnesiac participants, in the middle of a flawless performance, asked: "How am I doing this?" He had no awareness of how he was able to pick the correct object time and again—the knowledge was entirely nonconscious (Squire, 2012).

A significant additional piece of information is that such nonconscious, habitually formed cognition is also inflexible, meaning such cognition does not transfer into new contexts. This is demonstrated with a variation of the eight-pair matching task in which all sixteen objects are placed into one pile and the participant is asked to separate the objects into two piles—a correct and incorrect pile.

This task is easily accomplished by the unimpaired human subjects, in fact, once you've memorized the correct objects, sorting them into two piles is essentially the same task as identifying which object is the correct object within each pair. The amnesiacs, however, perform this sorting task with 50 percent accuracy—the percentage of chance. For the amnesiacs the knowledge of the correct objects is inflexible precisely because it has not been made conscious and can therefore not be transferred into a new context.

In a strange but true phenomenon known as "blind-sight," the same principle of inflexible nonconscious knowledge holds true. Blind-sight is a condition in which blind people can nevertheless register visual cues such as being able to mimic the direction of a light beam. What's most interesting and bizarre is those with blind sight do not consciously register the visual information and thus disregard evidence that they can in any way "see" the light beam. In contrast, those with normal vision register visual cues consciously and thus possess and access such information consciously (Koriat, 2000).

The greater takeaway here is that our ability to be in conscious control of our thinking via metacognition has evolved to increase cognitive performance. Metacognitive thinking is therefore essential for writing instruction. Metacognition facilitates the transfer of implicit cognition into explicit cognition where it can be stabilized for future performance as well as successfully transferred into different learning contexts.

WRITER-TEACHERS SPEAK TO METACOGNITION

Art Markman, a psychologist at the University of Texas at Austin, has spent decades studying the way our brains work. "We all have minds and very few of us have any idea how they work," he says, adding, "The more you know about the mind the more you can use it more effectively." This is the underlying argument of this chapter, namely, that the more you know about your writing process (i.e., metacognition) the better off you'll be as a writer. Likewise, the more you know about the ways in which you teach writing (i.e., metacognition) the better off you'll be as a teacher of writing.

William Olsen underlines this central idea that a metacognitive approach to writing is useful to writers as a way to learn more about their craft: "I rather like talk about poetry. That's part of what poetry offers, a subject to talk about. I like exchange about poetry and I don't mind talking about my own methods because it's one of the ways artists learn from each other."

Art Markman forwards the act of writing itself as a most useful heuristic toward developing metacognition, arguing that writing forces the writer to be explicit: "To really make sure you understand something try and explain it to somebody else or, better yet, just try and explain it to yourself. What that kind of explanation does is it forces you to be explicit about all of the details that you aren't normally that explicit about." Writing is itself a process of metacognition as writing surfaces and stabilizes thought.

Andrea Lunsford similarly asserts that "writing is epistemic." She explains, "It's not just the putting of knowledge down, it actually creates knowledge." This is the metacognitive process that Markman is speaking to, a process of making explicit what was inchoate or implicit. Writing is a primary vehicle for developing metacognition, for cultivating ideas into words. Mike Rose shares an illustrative example from his own experience:

> I remember that with finishing up *Lives on the Boundary*. I was reading some review of a book in *The New Yorker*, a novel, had nothing to do with nothing, it was just kind of, you know, leisurely, kind of looking at it, reading it and the reviewer used the word "capacious." The word just jumped out at me and goddamn it if I didn't end up using it in either the introduction or the conclusion. Not just using the word but everything the word represented. So that business of trying to present it, trying to frame it, engaging style, kind of bringing all the tools of craft to bear, that's a powerful dimension of writing and it's going on all the time and then there's the other stuff you're talking about where you're kind of writing yourself into something, trying to figure it out. To my mind they work in a kind of oscillation with each other.

This oscillation that Rose references is the productive oscillation of what is known and what is yet to be known. Writing is a medium through which to figure things out for oneself, to make connections and eventually to stabilize understandings with language. This is the benefit of metacognitive writing, of thinking thoughts through writing.

Andrea Lunsford speaks to the next concept—the value of acquiring metacognitive awareness of one's writing process. Lunsford references writers who are "choosing words that are coming into play there that they're not consciously aware of and don't want to be consciously aware of because they're afraid of messing something up."

This notion that some writers develop without metacognitive awareness, without the ability to translate their writing process into conscious awareness, serves as a warning. Ayn Rand (2000) spiritedly illustrates the point with this description of a writer lacking metacognitive awareness:

> He merely grasped the general idea of what writing is, then coasted on his subconscious for a while, never attempting to analyze where his ideas came from, what he was doing, or why. Such a writer is antagonistic to any analysis; he is the type who tells you that "the cold hand of reason'" is detrimental to his inspiration. He cannot function by means of reason, he says; if he begins to analyze, he feels, it will stop his inspiration altogether. (Given the way he functions, it would stop him.) (7)

As another famous example, here is Ernest Hemingway describing the lack of metacognitive awareness in F. Scott Fitzgerald:

> His talent was as natural as the pattern that was made by the dust on a butterfly's wings. At one time he understood it no more that the butterfly did and he did not know when it was brushed or marred. Later he became conscious of his damaged wings and of their construction and he learned to think and could not fly any more because the love of flight was gone and he could only remember when it had been effortless.

Writers who develop without metacognitive awareness are unable to adapt and transfer their writing abilities into new contexts while mystifying and imbuing the writing process with undue superstition. While a few writers may be able to get away with such an unreflective approach to writing, the writing teacher charged with parsing the writing process into manageable parts for adolescent learners certainly cannot.

As a final point from the testimonies of writer-teachers, it is clear that metacognition provides an overarching framework for one's writing life. Writer-teachers are well aware of their self-perceptions as writers and these self-perceptions provide a generative backdrop for their work.

Mariah Fredericks is a young-adult-fiction novelist who shares an in-depth, personal example:

> I'm thinking about writing process. The other thing that motivated me was that my dad was also writer. But he was an unhappy, disappointed person. He really never achieved what he wanted to achieve. And I always felt that for me knowing that I wanted to write—I've known I've wanted to write since I was a kid—I thought the only thing I can do is do my best to achieve it. I can't guarantee that I'm going to be a successful writer. But it was sort of a superstitious thing. If I write every single day, I will have tried my hardest. And I will have finished the book, and I will have tried my hardest. And if I send my book out, I will have done everything that I can to not feel like a failure if I don't get to do what I want to be doing for the rest of my life. He finished several books, and it was never enough for him. He didn't win this prize or he didn't have the kind of acclaim that other person . . . I mean, he set himself up against people . . . and I was really determined that I wasn't going to set up that kind of goal for myself.

In looking across testimonies from writer-teachers it is clear metacognition services writing in several ways. Metacognition enables writer-teachers to consciously develop elements of craft. Writer-teachers understand metacognition as the means through which implicit understandings become stabilized via language. Metacognition is also a tool by which to formulate and be able to rely on one's writing process over time. Finally, metacognitive awareness is a way of establishing a fertile landscape for one's extended writing life.

METACOGNITION AND TEACHING WRITING

When Michael Jordan, one of the most recognized basketball players in the history of the sport, was asked how he achieved so much on the basketball court he responded: "I just play." This attitude is terrific for playing but entirely antithetical to coaching. The shift from playing to coaching, from being a strong writer yourself to teaching adolescents to write, is a primary metacognitive move.

When I teach preservice teachers, for example, I explain they may be the worst candidates to teach their content since by virtue of being in a graduate-level course they have become masters of their content area and are therefore far removed from adolescent learners struggling to learn something new. These preservice teachers must learn to unpack how they learned in order to communicate effectively with adolescents.

This section on metacognition and the teaching of writing starts with you—with your experiences and ideas about writing—before offering strategies and approaches to cultivate a metacognitive-rich classroom for adolescent learners.

Teachers of Writing as Writers

Teachers of writing should be writers themselves. This does not mean they must be published authors or spend their evenings working on a novel but it does mean that teachers of writing should experience what it's like to invent, create, revise, and share writing with others. Thankfully this experience is more the rule than exception since writing has become more ubiquitous with the advent of writing-dependent technologies such as e-mail, text messaging, and social media platforms. In this regard writing is becoming more of a necessity in our culture, similar to what has happened with reading.

One immediate benefit of writing teachers experiencing writing first-hand is the cultivation of empathy and understanding the adolescent perspective. As we have seen throughout this book, writing is a cognitively demanding endeavor. Experiencing writing from the cockpit allows for a greater depth of identification when teaching writing.

Another immediate benefit of writing teachers experiencing writing firsthand is the ability to reflect on the writing process and share this with adolescent learners. This opens up the capacity to mentor the metacognitive thinking that accompanies writing. The following are some questions to consider for yourself when metacognitively reflecting on your own writing process:

- What does a successful writing session look like to you? What goals do you start with? Where do you end up?
- What are your writing habits and rituals? Do you write at certain times of day? Do you require any specific food or drink? Do you have a specific place for writing or need certain instruments?
- From where do the ideas for your writing usually come? Reading? Talking with others? Previous writing that you've done?
- Describe your revision process.
- How has your writing process changed over time?
- What do you most enjoy about writing? What is the hardest part about writing for you?
- What metaphor do you identify with writing?
- How do other people figure into your writing process? Do you share drafts at particular stages? Do you imagine certain audiences while writing?
- How do you know when a writing project is finished?

Interviewing Adolescent Writers

Adolescent writers are capable of answering their own metacognitive questions about writing. Table 7.1 provides a list of metacognitive interview questions to pose to adolescent writers:

Table 7.1.

Metacognitive Topic	Interview Questions
Personal history	How did you learn to write? What type of writing do you do outside of school?
The function of writing	Why do people write?
Writing strategies and qualities of good writing	What do you think a good writer needs to do in order to write well? How do your teachers decide which pieces of writing are the good ones?
Self-perceptions	What do you feel about what you've written so far? What do you most enjoy about writing? What is most difficult? What can I do to help you become a better writer?
Revision	What does it mean to revise? What is good revision as opposed to bad revision? What is your strategy for revision?
Conceptions of audience	How is your writing affected by who you think will be reading it? Do you think of your readers while writing?
Sense of completion	How do you determine when something you've written is finished?

These interview questions can take a variety of formats. For example, adolescent writers can write out their individual responses to these questions before sharing in small groups or whole-class discussion formats. Adolescent writers can also ask these interview questions of one another, taking interview notes of the responses they receive. Another format is one-on-one or small group teacher-student conferences.

No matter the format, a written record should be kept along with a follow-up mini-lecture or writing assignment to demonstrate these interview questions as formative assessments shaping future instruction. Action plans based on interview responses validate the metacognitive thinking shared by adolescent writers.

As an example of what can be gained from interviewing adolescent writers, one writing teacher—in response to the question of "What can I do to help you become a better writer?"—received this response: "Be honest with what I hand in. I don't need to know that what I wrote was great. I want to know what I can do better." Such a response helped this teacher open up a more critical and useful feedback space with adolescent writers.

As another example, one writing teacher changed tactics after the interview responses of adolescent writers placed too much emphasis on grades as the sole indicator of writing success. The adolescent writers downplayed their own judgments, indicating that grades were what told them if they were improving or writing well.

As a result, this writing teacher shares a newly implemented strategy: "I have been trying to get students in the habit of asking me one specific question (e.g., 'Did I explain my idea clearly here?') and also of telling me what they think of their own writing before I will offer my opinion." This writing teacher concludes, "I would like to see confidence in their writing improve independent of the grades received."

Metacognitive Writing Assignments

Asking adolescent writers to reflect, in writing, on their process is a direct and effective means of promoting metacognition. Metacognitive writing assignments are best completed in response to a specific piece of writing or set of writings. For every major writing assignment, for example, adolescents can be asked to add an additional paragraph in which they reflect on where they started with their ideas and how they eventually came to be formalized in their final written product.

Even deeper levels of reflection can be made when adolescent writers create sustained reflections alongside a portfolio of work. Here are some questions for adolescent writers that promote metacognitive reflection in response to a portfolio of writing:

- What differences do you see in your writing from the beginning of the process until now? What is the area you think you have improved the most? How do the writing pieces show your growth?
- What do you like about your writing in this portfolio? What would you improve?
- What challenges did you face in your writing so far? How did you overcome those challenges?
- What particular techniques did you adopt to improve yourself as a writer?
- What is your writing process? How has it changed?
- How did your writing benefit from peer feedback? How did your writing benefit from teacher feedback? How did you incorporate feedback?

- How did you choose the topics you wrote about? How are these topics important to you? How did your thinking on the topics evolve as you researched and wrote about them?
- What elements of your academic writing do you hope to improve in future classes? How will you apply certain skills in future classes? Will you continue to draft and revise if it is not required, for example?
- How have you applied what you have learned in this class to writing assignments in your other classes?
- Choose a metaphor to describe what writing is to you. Use that metaphor to explore how your approach to writing has evolved.
- How do you hope this portfolio of writing will represent you as a writer?

These questions promote sustained metacognitive writing on the part of adolescent writers. Table 7.2 provides two exceptional excerpts from adolescent writers reflecting on their writing portfolios:

Table 7.2.

Adolescent Writer #1	*Adolescent Writer #2*
Besides learning about how I wrote I also learned more about how I approached writing. I learned that writing is a cathartic process for me. It allows me to solidify thoughts that normally just float around in my brain. Whenever I get an assignment, I usually have a vague idea in my head of what I want to write. It's a little like a sneak preview of the perfect end product. Everything else I do after that is just me trying to achieve that perfection. Unfortunately, rarely do I ever obtain the degree of perfection my brain conjures up which leaves my inner critic very disappointed. However, my inner critic and I have come up with a peace treaty. Instead of the inner critic bashing everything I write as being too trite or unsubstantiated, she works with me. We start the writing process with cooperation, helping one another in achieving the ideal essay. When we fall short of that goal, we have also learned to be more forgiving and accept defeat as an opportunity to learn from our shortcomings.	My writing process has been to think until I know everything that I want to write down. This is a horrible process from experience as I am rarely able to begin writing. New thoughts are constantly being created and their relationships with existing thoughts only add on to the confusion. To address this issue, I would write down everything in mind. This often looks like a conversation to myself on paper but it works because I can manipulate which thoughts react with each other. I think of this as cooking, where I have to organize my spice rack so that I don't cook up a disaster.

Another metacognitive writing assignment successfully used with adolescent writers is to have adolescents interview writers about their process. Adolescents can interview friends or relatives about their writing habits or even contact an author they enjoy reading. There are also any number of published interviews with accomplished writers available that can be analyzed for the approaches writers take toward their craft.

Self-Monitoring and Self-Assessment

Positioning adolescent writers to be responsible for their own development through self-monitoring and self-assessment is a practice in metacognition. There are several ways to place adolescent writers at the center of their own development.

After adolescent writers receive feedback from teachers or peers, they should make a personalized action plan for revision. Keeping track of these action plans over time is a way to gain a longitudinal metacognitive view of writing development.

Another strategy requiring adolescent writers to self-assess is to have them turn in, along with the writing assignment, a completed rubric or a narrative justifying a particular grade or justifying the completeness of the assignment. When adolescent writers make a case that their writing satisfies the assignment description or rubric, they are thinking through the component parts of their writing—a practice in metacognition.

Adolescents can also be asked to create their own rubrics and assignment descriptions (chapter 1 speaks to this strategy as well). This metacognitive strategy gets adolescents to think about the writing assignment from a different perspective and results in a shared understanding about the requirements for a given writing assignment.

I recently attended a meeting with mentor teachers—those teachers taking on student teachers in their classrooms. One of the questions discussed had to do with what the mentor teachers would like to see their student teachers be able to do by the end of the year. One mentor teacher offered that she would like her student teacher to be able to "have students keep track of their own data." This is a tall order but a recognizably metacognitive task for adolescent learners. The strategies shared here are designed to enable adolescent writers to "keep track of their own data."

Teaching Adolescents to Read as Writers

Reading as a writer is a fundamental skill central to writing development and yet is rarely taught explicitly. Reading as a writer fits within this chapter on metacognition because it is principally a skill of making conscious what is experienced as a reader. We read and are affected by what we read. Sometimes we are even moved to action or frustration or empathy. The questions when reading as a writer become: How did the writer do that? What techniques did the writer use to create such an effect in the reader?

Reading as a writer is quintessentially different from reading as a reader. Just because you can ride a bicycle doesn't mean you know how to make one. Reading as a writer is about unpacking the writing to see how it's made so that you can construct your own creation utilizing the architectural techniques you have experienced as a reader.

Elizabeth Nunez speaks to the differences between reading as a reader and as a writer: "I read books that I love, that I forgot that I'm reading symbols, that I'm taken along on this journey. I suspend disbelief, I'm in another world. And then I read it again as a writer, and I say, 'How the heck did they do that?'" Stuart Dybek speaks to this separation between reading as a reader and writer as well:

> I think that most of the classes are about reading. One of the things I've noticed in my creative writing classes is that people come in there as very good readers and they want to talk about a piece of writing as readers and what I keep trying to get them to do is talk about it as a piece of writing, how it was made rather than what it means. You can't talk about something totally disregarding what it means but you can have your priorities.

In order to help adolescent writers read as writers, it becomes useful to set their priorities on "how it was made rather than what it means." The following set of questions are designed to place adolescent writers into this space where they are reading as writers:

- What genre is the writer working within? What are the indicators that tell you this is the genre?
- How is the text organized? Construct a diagram to illustrate the organizational structure of the text.
- What is the writer's purpose? How do you know?
- Who is the writer's intended audience? How do you know?
- What does this author do particularly well that you would like to add to your own writing toolbox?
- What might the author have done differently? What would you like to see explained in greater detail? Is there anything you would cut from the writing?
- Describe the language being employed by the writer. Academic? Informal? Wordy? Flowery? Impulsive? Measured? Sparse? Just right? Explain your description using illustrations from the writing.

- What does the writer use as evidence? (Quotations? Statistics? Anecdotes? A combination of these?) How effective is the overall evidence provided? What would be additionally effective?
- How does the writer transition between ideas? How does the writer transition between paragraphs?
- Pick out a line in the text that you think is working particularly well and explain your choice.

There are a few elements to note about this list of questions. First, the questions themselves move from global to more local analyses of the writing. Second, the choice of text to be read and analyzed as a writer is of critical importance. I prefer to use strong models from adolescent writers, usually students from a prior class, to do this type of analysis. A strong adolescent text will be more accessible than a published writer and more open to critique. There is, however, certainly a place to read as a writer with published materials too. I just wouldn't necessarily start there.

The end goal of reading as a writer (and the most rewarding) is to steal strategies for yourself. Diane Seuss shares, "When I read somebody who really rocks my boat I want to, not ape them, but integrate the thing that I see there, that I think, 'Oh I need to try that.'" Reading as a writer is a powerful strategy of recognizing your reactions to a given text and arriving at an understanding of how the author is able to provoke these reactions.

Teaching Adolescents about the Brain

Teaching adolescents about their own brains is a metacognitive strategy for writing instruction. A place to begin teaching adolescents about the brain is to introduce a number of "neuromyths" (see table 7.3) grounded in popular opinion but little else alongside the actual stories grounded in brain science.

Debunking neuromyths with facts supported by brain science begins metacognitive conversations with adolescent writers about the brain. Adolescents ought to be encouraged to share any facts they have come to hold about the brain and to research whether or not these preconceived notions are grounded in fact, myth, or some combination thereof.

Empowering facts about the brain that should be shared with adolescent learners is what we know about the adolescent brain, namely, that adolescent brains are highly malleable, which is a great thing for learning, especially learning to write. The adolescent brain is, in fact, primed for learning. Here I will refer you back to the introduction of this book, which goes into greater detail about the adolescent brain, highlighting

Table 7.3.

Neuromyth	The Real Story
The bigger your brain, the smarter you are.	As highlighted in the opening of this book, intelligence is all about the connections the brain makes, not the size of the brain.
We only use 10 percent of our brains.	Popularized in film and television, this myth holds no truth. We use our entire brain.
The right hemisphere of the brain is for emotion and creativity while the left hemisphere is for logic and reasoning.	Emotion, creativity, logic, reasoning—these are all higher-order thinking skills that require the whole brain.
There are critical periods of brain development and if these are missed, there is no hope of developing certain skills such as learning a new language or how to play a musical instrument.	This myth is especially pernicious since it holds some truth, namely, that there are certain sensitive periods of brain development. The complete story, however, is that we can continue to learn and change our brain architecture throughout our lives.
By age three you have all the neurons you'll ever have.	We now know that neurogenesis—the creation of new neurons in the brain—continues well into adolescence and adulthood.
Brain games can make you smarter and keep your brain young.	Brain games are certainly not going to cause you any harm but they are also not going to keep your brain young or make you smarter in anything but the games themselves. There is little transferability between brain games and other forms of cognition.
Brain damage is permanent.	Brain plasticity is remarkable, especially in response to trauma.
Vaccines cause cognitive disorders such as autism.	There is no scientific evidence to support this myth.
You have a specific learning style such as visual, auditory, or kinesthetic.	The truth is that all of us learn through various modes. This is why differentiating delivery styles in the classroom works for all adolescent learners.
Sugar reduces attention.	A commonly held belief with no scientific support.
Learning problems are lasting and cannot be improved by education.	Education has been shown to demonstrably improve and even overcome learning problems.
Multitasking is a sign of intelligence.	Multitasking results in doing two or more things poorly (think about the dangers associated with texting and driving, for example). A better sign of intelligence is concentrating on doing one thing well rather than dividing your attention among several competing tasks.

the development of the prefrontal cortex and the preponderance of white matter in the brain alongside decreasing gray matter.

Finally, the major concepts that serve as hubs to each chapter in this book can be shared explicitly with adolescent writers. The depth of description you choose is of course linked to the learners in your classroom and the potential relevance to your curriculum. Table 7.4 overviews the brain concepts introduced in this book along with abbreviated definitions and relationships to the writing process that can be shared with adolescent writers.

This table also services a secondary function—to review the major concepts presented in this book. This is where we've been. Where we're going is up to you and how you best see fit to integrate the arguments, concepts, and strategies offered here into your own teaching and writing.

Table 7.4.

Brain Concept	Definition	Relationship to the Writing Process
Automaticity	The ability to accomplish physical and cognitive tasks easily and effortlessly as a result of practice and learning.	Just like perfecting a tennis stroke or basketball shot, the more you practice writing the more automatic and effortless the process of writing becomes.
Theory of Mind	Our ability to know what is going on in other people's minds and to reason about the beliefs of others and ourselves.	Conceptualizing audience—others and ourselves—is a practice in theory of mind, a practice in thinking through the perspective of your readers.
Brain States	Like a computer running different software programs, our brains weave in and out of different brain states.	Writing is a complex skill set requiring various brain states. Invention and editing stages of the writing process, for example, require different states of mind.
Brain Variation	Brain variation is the rule, not the exception. We all have different brains as a result of different experiences, genetics, and ways of seeing the world.	Writing is a medium in which brain variation is on full display. Writing expresses our individuality and highlights our unique ways of seeing and thinking.
Positive Affect	Positive affect refers to being in a healthy, optimistic state of mind, which improves cognition.	Brain research on positive affect points to something we have intuitively known for a long time: We are better at things we enjoy. Having fun with writing will make your writing better and make you a better writer in the long run.
Nonconscious Cognition	Nonconscious cognition is mental work completed outside of conscious awareness.	Nonconscious cognition is intimately tied to the writing process and includes writing to discover and deferring conscious awareness. The sophisticated, mature writer is marked by an ability to balance between conscious and nonconscious cognition within the writing process.
Metacognition	Metacognition is cognition about cognition or thinking about how we think.	Thinking and writing about writing helps to stabilize the writing process which leads to better writing and transferability (the ability to take what you have learned in one place and apply it to another place).

References

Beeman, Mark. (2014). Interdisciplinary international symposium on creativity. Banbury Center, Cold Spring Harbor Laboratory.

Bizzaro, Patrick. (2010). Personal interview (March 8).

Blakemore, Sarah-Jayne. (2012). TEDxGlobal 2012: The mysterious workings of the adolescent brain.

Bogin, Barry. (1999). Evolutionary perspective on human growth. *Annual Review of Anthropology* 28: 109–53.

Brandt, Deborah. (2010). Personal interview (November 12).

Buckner, Randy L. (2012). The serendipitous discovery of the brain's default network. *Neuroimage* 62(2): 1137–45.

Choi, Charles Q. (2009). Being more infantile may have led to bigger brains. *Scientific American.* June 15.

Common Core State Standards. (n.d.). English language arts writing standards, grades 11–12. Retrieved from www.corestandards.org/ELA-Literacy/W/11-12.

Damasio, Antonio. (1994). *Descartes' Error: Emotion, Reason, and the Human Brain.* New York: Penguin Books.

Darwin, Charles. (2010, originally published 1887). *The Autobiography of Charles Darwin.* Pacific Publishing Studio. Seattle, Washington.

Dybek, Stuart. (2008). Personal interview (April 28).

Ebert, T., C. Wienbruch, B. Rockstroh, and E. Taub. (1995). Increased cortical representation of the fingers of the left hand in string players. *Science* 270: 305–7.

Elbow, Peter. (2012). Personal interview (August 30).

Fink, Andreas, Barbara Graif, Aljoscha C. Neubauer. (2009). Brain correlates underlying creative thinking: EEG alpha activity in professional vs. novice dancers. *Neuroimage* 46: 854–62.

Fitzgerald, F. Scott. (1936). The crack-up. *Esquire*. (February).

Fredericks, Mariah. (2013). Personal interview conducted by Sarah O'Hare (January 13).

Fu, Danling. (2009). *Writing between Languages: How English Language Learners Make the Transition to Fluency*. Portsmouth, NH: Heinemann.

Galbraith, David. (1999). Writing as a knowledge-constituting process. In M. Torrance and David Galbraith (eds.), *Studies in Writing*, vol. 4, *Knowing What to Write: Conceptual Processes in Text Production* (139–60). Amsterdam: Amsterdam University Press.

Gee, James. (2010). Personal interview (August 3).

Greene, Brenda. (2013). Personal interview conducted by Blanche Mackey-Williams (June 28).

Greene, Terry R., and Helga Noice. (1988). Influence of positive affect upon creative thinking and problem solving in children. *Psychological Reports* 63: 895–98.

Hemingway, Ernest. (1964). *A Moveable Feast*. New York: Scribner.

Higginbotham, Adam. (2013). Personal interview (February 5).

Irish, George. (2013). Personal interview conducted by Blanche Mackey-Williams (June 28).

James, William. (1890). *Principles of Psychology*, vol. 1. New York: Dover Publications.

Kandel, Eric. (n.d.). Identical twins, not identical brains. Retrieved from www.dnalc.org/view/1200-Identical-Twins-Not-Identical-Brains.html.

Kerlikowske, Elizabeth. (2008). Personal interview (April 9).

Komunyakaa, Yusef. (2008). Personal interview (October 22).

Koriat, Asher. (2000). The feeling of knowing: Some metatheoretical implications for consciousness and control. *Consciousness and Cognition* 9: 149–71.

Lahiri, Jhumpa. (2013). Unknown territory: An interview with Jhumpa Lahiri. Interview conducted by Cressida Leyshon. *The New Yorker*. October 18, 2013.

Laing, Lucy. (2014). "Little miracle" Jake Gladstone defying the doctors despite being born with half his brain missing. *Mirror online*. Retrieved from www.mirror.co.uk.

Lauer, Janice. (2010). Personal interview (January 27).

Limb, Charles J., and Allen R. Braun. (2008). Neural substrates of spontaneous musical performance: An fMRI study of jazz improvisation. *PLos ONE* 3(2): e1679.

Lindquist, Julie. (2010). Personal interview (January 4).

Loeb, Susanna, James Soland, and Lindsay Fox. (2014). Is a good teacher a good teacher for all? Comparing value-added of teachers with their English learners and non-English learners. *Education Evaluation and Policy Analysis* 36(4): 457–75.

Lunsford, Andrea. (2012). Personal interview (September 2).

Luria, Alexander. (1987). *The Mind of a Mnemonist: A Little Book about a Vast Memory.* Cambridge, MA: Harvard University Press.

Maguire, Eleanor A., David G. Gadian, Ingrid S. Johnsrude, Catriona D. Good, John Ashburner, Richard S. J. Frackowiak, and Christopher D. Frith. 2000. Navigation- related structural change in the hippocampi of taxi drivers. *Proc. Natl. Acad. Sci. USA* 97(8): 4398–4403.

Markman, Art. (2013). Personal interview (May 20).

Maxwell, Richard. (2013). Personal interview conducted by David Allen (March 21).

Milner, Brenda. (1998). Brenda Milner. In Larry Squire (ed.), *The History of Neuroscience in Autobiography* (278–305). San Diego, CA: Academic Press.

Nunez, Elizabeth. (2013). Personal interview conducted by Casandra Murray (March 20).

Olsen, William. (2008). Personal interview (April 11).

Perani, Daniela, Eraldo Paulesu, Nuria Sebastian Galles, Emmanuel Dupoux, Stanislad Dehaene, Valentino Bettinardi, Stefano F. Cappa, Ferruccio Fazio, and Jacques Mehler. (1998). The bilingual brain: Proficiency and age of acquisition of the second language. *Brain* 121: 1841–52.

Perl, Sondra. (2011). Personal interview (April 4).

Pfeifer, Jennifer, Matthew D. Lieberman, and Mirella Dapretto. (2007). "I know you are but what am I?!": Neural bases of self- and social knowledge retrieval in children and adults. *Journal of Cognitive Neuroscience* 19(8): 1323–37.

Pinker, Steven. (1994). *The Language Instinct: How the Mind Creates Language.* New York: Harper Collins.

Ramachandran, V. S. (2011). *The Tell-Tale Brain: A Neuroscientist's Quest for What Makes Us Human.* New York: W. W. Norton.

Rand, Ayn. (2000). *The Art of Fiction: A Guide for Writers and Readers.* New York: Penguin.

Rose, Mike. (2010). Personal interview (February 14).

Seuss, Diane. (2008). Personal interview (July 8).

Siegal, Michael, and Rosemary Varley. (2002). Neural systems involved in "theory of mind." *Nature Reviews Neuroscience* 3 (June).

Sommers, Nancy. (2012). Personal interview (September 5).

Sousa, David A. (2011). *How the Brain Learns.* Thousand Oaks, CA: Corwin Press.

Squire, Larry. (2012). Interdisciplinary symposium on literature, memory and neuroscience. Banbury Center, Cold Spring Harbor Laboratory.

Stickgold, Robert. (2014). Interdisciplinary international symposium on creativity. Banbury Center, Cold Spring Harbor Laboratory.

_____. (2013). Personal interview (August 7).

Tanenbaum, Leora. (2012). Personal interview (February 8).

Wakoski, Diane. (2007). Personal interview (August 22).

White, Simone. (2013). Personal interview conducted by Sarah O'Hare (April 27).

Wilhelm, Jeffrey. (2007). Imagining a new kind of self: Academic language, identity, and content area learning. *Voices from the Middle* 15: 1.

Wilson, Edward O. (1999). *Consilience: The Unity of Knowledge*. New York: Random House.

Wilson, Timothy. (2002). *Strangers to Ourselves: Discovering the Adaptive Unconscious*. Cambridge, MA: Harvard University Press.

Wirtz, Jason. (2012). Writing courses live and die by the quality of peer review. In K. Hunzer (ed.), *Collaborative Learning and Writing: Essays on Using Small Groups in Teaching English and Composition* (5–16). Jefferson, NC: McFarland.

Yang, Gene. (2011). Personal interview (February 9).

Yoo, Julie J., Oliver Hinds, Noa Ofen, Todd W. Thompson, Susan Whitfield-Gabrieli, Christina Triantafyllou, John D. E. Gabrieli. (2012). When the brain is prepared to learn: Enhancing human learning using real-time fMRI. *NeuroImage* 59: 846–52.

Index

invention (brain state), 40–41, 43, 90, 92, 94, 97

James, William, 1
Jeopardy (game), 74
Journey of the Imagination (exercise), 95–96
Joyce, James, 37
Just Ask (writing activity), 82

Kandel, Eric, 51
Kerlikowske, Elizabeth, 4, 98
knowledge-constituting (writing model), 101–02
Komunyakaa, Yusef, 90–93, 98, 103
K-W-L (activity/exercise), 6

Lahiri, Jhumpa, 57
Lauer, Janice, vii, 3–4
Learning Disabled (LD). *See* special needs learners
Lindquist, Julie, 90
Lives on the Boundary (Rose), 109
Lunsford, Andrea, viii, 21, 92, 109–10
Luria, Alexander, 87
Lyon, George Ella, 10

Magnetic Poetry (language activity), 79
making predictions (WTL activity), 24
MAPS (acrostic), 11–12
Markman, Art, 37, 71, 91, 102, 109
memory, formation/retention/loss, *1.1*, 35–36, 85–87, 89, 107
mentors/mentoring, xii, 101, 112, 116
metacognition:
    chapter overview, xiv, 106–07;
    debunking neuromyths, 118–20;
    defined/described, 121;
    experiments/studies, 107–08;
    importance of teachers as writers, 111–12;
    interview questions, 113–14;
    perspectives, teacher/writer, 109–11;
    reading as a writer, 116–18;

writing assignments, reflections on, 114–16;
    writing assignments, self-assessment, 116
metaphor, use of:
    brain states, 34;
    connection to Common Core, 49;
    nonconscious cognition, 90–94;
    what writing is, 112, 115
Meyer, Stephenie, 71
Milner, Brenda, 85–86
mind, brain, and education (MBE), xi
The Mind at Work (Rose), 3
mind-reading, 25
mixed language writing (ELL activity), 59
Mixing, Balancing, Perfect Ratio (metaphor), 93–94
models/modeling:
    Apprentice Writing, 10, 80;
    connection to Common Core, 66;
    dual-process, 101–02;
    feedback, 55–56;
    inductive vs. deductive teaching, 64;
    Teacher Talk-Aloud, 9;
    teaching ELL, 58–59;
    teaching special needs, 61;
    using students as, 118;
    whole class, 59–60
Molaison, Henry, 85–86, 108

natural writer. *See* high-performing writers
negative affective states (stress/anxiety), 68–69
neuromyths, *119*
neuron connections/neurogenesis, x–xii, xiii, 3, 46, 119
nonconscious cognition:
    chapter overview, xiv, 84–85, 105;
    Common Core connection, 103–05;
    core concept of teaching, viii;
    defined/described, 84–85, 121;
    experiments/studies, 85–89;
    perspectives, teacher/writer, 90–94;

About the Author

A former high school English teacher, Jason Wirtz is associate professor of English Education and Rhetoric & Composition at Hunter College, City University of New York. His research focuses on translating the practices of accomplished writer-teachers for secondary and postsecondary writing instruction.